Believing is Seeing
the Gift of Faith

a missionary's journey to
faith that moves mountains

Caroline Chesnutt

BELIEVING PRAYER: THE GIFT OF FAITH

A missionary's journey
to faith that moves mountains

Caroline Chesnutt

RHEMA
PUBLISHING HOUSE
www.RhemaPublishingHouse.com

For ordering information contact https://carolinechesnutt.com/

Published by
RHEMA Publishing House.™
rhemapublishinghouse.com
PO Box 1244 McKinney, TX 75070

All scriptures are from the New King James Version unless otherwise
noted.

Scripture taken from the NEW KING JAMES VERSION®. Copyright©
1980 by Thomas Nelson, Inc. Used by permission. All rights reserved.

Cover photo by http://www.justinongleyphotography.com/

Interior and cover design by Lee Desmond

ISBN: paper 978-0-9990932-8-3
ISBN: ebook 978-0-9990932-9-0

This book is dedicated to:

God, my Father;

The Holy Spirit, my Teacher;

Jesus, the Author and Finisher of my faith;

Cornerstone Nashville, my church home;

Sandi Aldridge, my friend, mentor, and sister in Christ;

And my mother—my cheerleader & biggest fan.

Contents

Preface

It has been said, "An ounce of believing is worth more than a ton of asking." I believe this to be true. Through the years, God has unexpectedly used many different lives all across the globe to leave an indelible mark on my soul; to teach me about faith, hope, and love; to teach me about Himself. These are the stories of those beautiful lives. All the stories are true. They are firsthand accounts of what I have seen and experienced.

My faith is far from perfect; I am still growing, God is still teaching. But this is the story of my journey from Asking to Believing. This is my journey of faith.

CHAPTER ONE

ASKING PRAYER

If you have faith the size of a mustard seed, you will say to this mountain, "Move from here to there," and it will move; and nothing will be impossible for you.
Matthew 17:20

My younger years were spent on the foreign mission field, with a heart full of love and zeal, searching for a deeper, more powerful faith in the God whom I adored. I had faith. After all, I left my home and family and moved halfway around the world because of that faith! But somehow, I knew there was a faith out there that was so strong and so deep that it could truly move mountains...

Oh no. Why is this man coming to my table for help!? It's obvious his pitiful condition is permanent and there is nothing I can do—well, of course if God wanted to, He could do a miracle—but that never happens!

Those were my thoughts that sunny South American day, sitting in the medical tent with the other American doctors, nurses, and dentists. We had all traveled here with Health Teams International to this tiny mountain village to bring the Good News of the Gospel: that Jesus Saves—as well as plenty of free vitamins, Tylenol, worm medicine, toothbrushes, eyeglasses, and dental work.

I watched him slowly make his way towards me, and my heart broke. As a young, handsome man in his 30s, he should have been in his prime. Yet here he was, dragging himself across the dirty floor on a cardboard box. His legs were shriveled up and contracted beneath his body. He crawled over to where I was sitting at a table with a student nurse. Because he was unable to sit in a chair, we both knelt on the ground next to him and listened to his sad story:

He had contracted polio as an infant; his paralyzed legs had never worked, he had never stood on his own a day in his life. When he heard we were coming, he had traveled for three days, sometimes crawling, sometimes riding on the back of motorcycles—all because of *faith*—his faith in the Americans. He believed we had a magic cure for his disease, and somehow, if he could just reach us, he would be a cripple no longer. Being uneducated, this poor man didn't realize just how impossible his request was. Perhaps that made it a little easier for him to believe. But there is no cure for polio. Paralyzed legs do not regain strength. And no amount of vitamins and Tylenol would do anything for this crippled man, except relieve a little soreness.

I didn't want to pray for healing. I knew I didn't have faith to believe God would actually do it, so I didn't even want to ask. It's better not to try at all, than to try and fail and look like an idiot, right!? It's easy to pray for things that have a halfway decent chance of happening anyway! We do that all the time. But praying for the impossible takes

Believing Prayer, and a faith much bolder than mine was. Also, I didn't want to shame or embarrass God.

> *But bold faith, though it may embarrass people, doesn't ever shame God. Sin does.*

Instead, I gave him vitamins and Tylenol and escorted him to the prayer tent, where Rocky, a fiery, faith-filled, tongue-talking, spirit-led evangelist was happy to oblige. My team members and I watched as Rocky shared Christ with this man and explained God's plan for salvation—by sending His only son to pay for the redemption of sinful man with His death. He also explained that Jesus Christ is the Healer, and by faith we can be healed because He not only took our sin, He also took our sickness and diseases on the cross (Matthew 8:17). Rocky opened the Bible and read Acts 3, where Peter says to the crippled man:

In the name of Jesus Christ of Nazareth, get up and walk.
Acts 3:6

Just as if we were living in a scene from the book of Acts, Rocky said those words to the crippled man: "In the name of Jesus Christ of Nazareth, get up and walk." The man replied, "I have never stood in my life." Rocky repeated the command: "In the name of Jesus Christ of Nazareth, get up and walk." This time, the man slowly began to stretch his shriveled, paralyzed legs beneath him and stood!

There was no sudden clap of thunder; no flashing neon lights, announcing that an amazing miracle was about to occur. It just quietly happened. The crippled man was simply standing tall in the middle of the yard, holding on to nothing, and nobody was assisting him, or even touching him. He just stood up all by himself on those skinny little legs and slowly began to walk, with a giant grin on his face and tears filling his eyes. His faith had healed him, just as Jesus promised in the Bible. He came to us that day with the faith to be healed. He just needed to put that faith in the Great Physician, instead of the Americans.

Asking Prayer

While serving God overseas, when faced with a difficult, impossible, or simply overwhelming need, I would sometimes find myself saying, "Well, we can go to God in prayer. All we can do is ask." Really!?! Is that *all* we can do?!?

Asking Prayer is rooted in Hope: It asks and hopes to receive.

Asking Prayer asks, and keeps on asking, prays and keeps on praying—sometimes pleading or making promises—desperately hoping to receive what it seeks. "Pray until something happens" is the adage. I am very familiar with this kind of prayer. It was all I knew for most of my Christian life. It is not bad or wrong. It is very good and very necessary. In fact, we are told several times in the Bible, to make our requests known to God:

> *Be anxious for nothing, but in everything*
> *by prayer and supplication, with thanksgiving,*
> *let your requests be made known to God.*
> Philippians 4:6

How else are we supposed to let our needs be made known to God, but by asking Him to meet them? And then asking Him again, and again, and again—and as many times as it takes until we finally receive what we're asking for. Many saints have worked wonders through this type of persistent, unrelenting Asking Prayer. Jesus Himself encourages us to pray like this with ceaseless, heartfelt prayers, just like the persistent widow:

> *There was in a certain city a judge who did not fear God*
> *nor regard man. Now there was a widow in that city;*
> *and she came to him, saying "Get justice for me from my*
> *adversary." And he would not for awhile, but afterward*
> *he said within himself, "Though I do not fear God nor*
> *regard man, yet because this widow troubles me I will*
> *avenge her, lest by her continual coming she weary me."*
> *Hear what the unjust judge said. And shall God not avenge*
> *His own elect who cry out day and night to Him,*
> *though he bears long with them?*
> Luke 18:2-7

However, it is curious that the very next verse seems to question the level of faith of God's own elect, who "cry out day and night" in persistent Asking Prayers:

> *I tell you that He will avenge them speedily.*
> *Nevertheless, when the Son of Man comes, will*
> *He really find faith on the earth?*
> Luke 18:8

—or we can pray like the noisy neighbor, who persistently asked for bread at midnight:

> *Which of you shall have a friend, and go to him at*
> *midnight and say to him, "Friend, lend me three loaves;*
> *for a friend of mine has come to me on his journey, and*
> *I have nothing to set before him," and he will answer*
> *from within and say, "Do not trouble me; the door is now*
> *shut, and my children are with me in bed; I cannot rise*
> *and give to you?" I say to you, though he will not rise and*
> *give to him because he is his friend, yet because of his*
> *persistence he will rise and give him as many as he needs.*
> *I say to you, ask and it will be given to you; seek and you*
> *will find; knock and it will be opened to you.*
> Luke 11:5-9

Just like the noisy neighbor knocking in the night, we are told to be persistent and ask, seek, and knock. God rewards his children who come diligently looking for Him, day and night; who never stop knocking, asking for their needs to be met. So, God the Father can then rise, give them everything they need, and fulfill ALL the desires of their hearts, as they delight themselves in Him (Psalm 37:4).

Let's Make a Deal

I imagine almost all Christians (and probably a great many non-Christians) have at some time in their lives prayed to "make a deal" with God. I know I did many times as a young girl, dreaming of dolls and ponies. My favorite example of making promises to God and wearing Him out with persistent Asking Prayers is the beautiful story of Hannah (1 Sam 1).

Hannah was childless and longing for a son for many years. She asked repeatedly in hopes that God would grant her request. She went every day to the temple and begged God for a son, with tears and sorrow and many prayers. The Bible says she was in "bitterness of soul" and "wept in anguish" (1 Sam 1:10). Her prayers were so passionate and persistent that Eli, the high priest at the time, thought she was drunk! She finally became desperate enough to "make a deal" with God. She made a solemn promise to the Lord: if He would only give her a son, she would dedicate that child back to Him for a lifetime of service in the Temple (1 Sam 1:11). God rewarded her persistent Asking Prayers and her vow, made in "bitterness of soul." He gave her a son. And not just any son! Hannah's child was Samuel, one of the greatest prophets of all time.

God hears persistent, unrelenting Asking Prayer, and He answers. And so, like Hannah, we ask and keep on asking; we seek and keep on seeking; we knock and keep on knocking.

Heartsick Hannah

Hannah's story is a good example of the meaning of this Proverb:

> *Hope deferred makes the heart sick,*
> *but when desire comes, it is a tree of life.*
> Proverbs 13:12

While her biological clock was ticking, her female rival was mocking, and her future "tree of life" was hanging in the balance, Hannah was struggling year after year to keep her deferred hope alive in her deep desire for a baby boy. Her poor heart was surely sick! She was so deeply grieved and in such sorrow of soul, that she was *miserable*. She cried all the time and would not even eat.

Hannah wasn't exactly the picture of a joyful saint, filled with faith and hope, confidently waiting on the promises of God! I would say, she was more like a desperate damsel in deep distress whose only hope and prayer was God—which is certainly better than no hope at all! Nevertheless, she hammered heaven's gates with ceaseless prayers day and night. When her desire finally arrived, she gave the child back to God. She also offered a beautiful prayer of thanksgiving and exaltation to God, a fitting and joyful response for hopes realized and faith fulfilled. A prayer of praise worth imitating:

> *My heart rejoices in the Lord; my horn is exalted*
> *in the Lord. I smile at my enemies,*
> *because I rejoice in Your salvation.*

*No one is holy like the Lord, for there is none besides You,
nor is there any rock like our God. Talk no more so very
proudly; let no arrogance come from your mouth,
for the Lord is the God of knowledge; and by Him actions
are weighed. The bows of the mighty men are broken,
and those who stumbled are girded with strength.
Those who were full have hired themselves out for bread,
and the hungry have ceased to hunger. Even the barren
has borne seven, and she who has many children has
become feeble. The Lord kills and makes alive; He brings
down to the grave and brings up, the Lord makes poor
and makes rich; He brings low and lifts up. He raises the
poor from the dust and lifts the beggar from the ash heap,
to set them among princes and make them inherit the
throne of glory...*
I Samuel 2:1-8

*Asking Prayer works.
It moves the mighty heart of God to act on behalf
of His children.*

This is why we pray—for ourselves and our loved ones; for health and deliverance; jobs and finances; safety and security; lost friends and ruined relationships. We keep on praying, asking, and making our lists; dropping to our knees to bring our needs again and again into the Throne Room of God. Because we know He hears us, and we hope He will "avenge us speedily"—bringing with Him prayers perfected, desires delivered, and longings satisfied. When He does, we (like Hannah) rightly respond in joyful gratitude, with thanks and praise.

On the other hand, sometimes life can be brutal. It has a funny way of beating us down; of leaching our faith and draining our hope. In times like these, prayer grows dry and bitter. If we are even able to pray at all, Asking Prayer really is all that we can do. We ask and keep on asking; hope and keep on hoping; just trying hard to keep faith and hope alive a little while longer.

When we finally see the answer from Heaven, and our long-awaited desire arrives, then it will be a joyful tree of life. But until that day, like Hannah, we wait. And month after month, year after year, our hope is long deferred. Our hearts grow sick. Our faith grows weak, and it takes everything we've got to muster the courage one more time: to ask and keep on asking—even with sorrow and weeping and fasting.

And sometimes, when life-altering trials come our way, we are taken by surprise. Fear, weakness, and doubts prevail. We may be suddenly faced with impossible situations (like a crippled man who wants to walk!) which can leave us speechless and helpless. When this happens, we may not have the faith to ask God for the impossible. Because Asking Prayer seems pointless when you have no faith to believe. Why should we even ask!??

This is where Believing Prayer steps in . . .

CHAPTER TWO

BELIEVING PRAYER

Therefore I say to you, whatever things you ask when you pray, believe that you receive them, and you will have them.
Mark 11:24

I was sitting at a tiny table with a brilliantly talented American critical care physician, Dr. Don, who teaches medicine at a teaching hospital in an ICU setting. We were both a little tired after seeing patients all week in a sweaty makeshift village clinic. We were serving together with Health Teams, deep in the jungles of Myanmar.

A lovely, middle-aged Burmese woman came and sat before us. She smiled and shared that she had just heard the gospel and accepted Jesus Christ as her Lord and Savior. We smiled back, saying we were happy for her. Dr. Don then asked how we could help her physically. At that very moment, before she could even reply, she gasped, grabbed her chest, collapsed on the ground, vomited all over the floor, eyes rolled back, and became unconscious.

As an ICU nurse working with an ICU doctor, we acted fast and had a pretty good idea of what was going on. Dr. Don confirmed my suspicions; these were the classic, textbook symptoms of a massive posterior myocardial infarction (a huge heart attack). Not a good prognosis, even if we had been in a top-level facility in America.

I grabbed what little equipment we had and quickly took her vital signs. She was barely breathing. Her pulse was 38 and very weak. Her blood pressure was 45/20 (which is not nearly enough to support any major organs in the body—the brain, lungs, and heart). We had a finger probe to measure her oxygen. It was reading 70% and dropping. This was not good. We had nothing to give her: no oxygen, no rescue drugs, no morphine, no ventilator—nothing. We were in the middle of the jungle in a 3rd world country, hours away from civilization with zero hope of an ambulance ever arriving. Even with CPR, her chances of survival were slim to none. Realizing this woman's death was imminent, Dr. Don looked out the window in desperation and prayed that oxygen would somehow miraculously arrive on the wind blowing through the trees.

This would be the first death our mission team would experience at any of our outreaches, and a very bad omen in the village people's eyes! Because she had appeared to be healthy when she came to us, they would likely blame us for her death—forbid anyone from visiting our clinic, forbid us from ever returning—or even worse!

The local Burmese believers who were working with us, insisted we let them take over her care. Not wanting to offend them with their unique cultural methods of dealing with death, we agreed. They carried her limp body into a back room. A few minutes later, curiosity got the best of me. I snuck into the room to see what was happening to the dying woman. The Burmese believers were gathered around her bed fervently praying Believing Prayers. Some were praying in English, some in Burmese, and some in Pentecostal tongues. They anointed her with oil and declared out loud that she would not die, but live and be completely healed!

Each time I snuck in, she appeared to be barely alive. She was unconscious, pale and cold; taking minimal, short breaths. They continued their fervent prayer and anointing for about 30-45 minutes. Meanwhile, Dr. Don and I went back to work in the clinic. Then, one of the Burmese believers came out of the room smiling. He approached and asked if we would see the woman in the back room. We entered the room and were surprised and thrilled to see the dying woman sitting up on the side of the bed, smiling and laughing and drinking a glass of water! She spoke to us of visions of Jesus and angels which she had seen while she was almost dead. She was very excited, waving her arms, yelling and praising God.

Dr. Don assessed her, and there were no signs of cardiac distress or any residual symptoms of the heart attack she just had. There was no pain or shortness of breath. She was the picture of perfect health, as if nothing had happened. Only a few short hours after her heart attack, this joyful newborn believer walked out of our clinic rejoicing in the God who saves.

And the prayer of faith shall save the sick,
and the Lord will raise him up.
James 5:15

It was truly a miracle. The prayer of faith (the Believing
Prayer) of the Burmese believers had saved the sick and dying
woman, and the Lord had raised her up. . .right before our eyes.

Believing Prayer

Believing Prayer is the prayer of faith. It does not rely on persistent, unrelenting asking to bend God's ear. Rather, it relies on simple unwavering, unshakable faith that if He said it, He will do it—end of story. There is no conversation. There is no room for doubt. If He said it's going to happen, it is going to happen. Period.

Similar to Asking Prayer, Believing Prayer can also be seen in the Biblical metaphor of the neighbor knocking on the door at midnight. However, when Believing Prayer comes to the door, it knocks not as the persistent noisy neighbor, but *as the trusting child*. It comes as the child who is so deeply loved and cherished by the Father, it's as if he were the only child—and he knows it! The neighbor *knocks in hope* that the door will open, and he is determined to keep on knocking louder and louder until it finally does open. But the child softly *knocks in faith* and knows beyond a shadow of doubt that the door will definitely open for him—because after all, it is his Father's house.

My house shall be called a house of prayer for all nations.
Isaiah 56:7

Believing Prayer is rooted in Faith:
It believes and waits in faith to receive.

Believing Prayer asks in faith, fully believing; then with joy and thanksgiving, positions itself with anticipation, ready to receive what is requested. This Believing Prayer—this simple faith that simply asks, then believes and stands ready to receive—is so powerful and so persuasive, that **even Jesus was amazed** when He encountered it on earth:

*Now when Jesus had entered Capernaum, a centurion came to Him, pleading with Him, saying "Lord, my servant is lying at home paralyzed, dreadfully tormented." And Jesus said to him, "I will come and heal him." The centurion answered and said, "Lord, I am not worthy that You should come under my roof. But only speak a word and my servant will be healed. For I also am a man under authority, having soldiers under me. And I say to this one, "Go" and he goes; and to another "Come" and he comes; and to my servant "Do this" and he does it. When Jesus heard it, **He marveled**, and said to those who followed, "Assuredly, I say to you, I have not found such great faith, not even in Israel!"*
Matthew 8:5-10 (emphasis mine)

The centurion asked only once. His simple Believing Prayer didn't require a big production, or even that Jesus should enter his home. He just asked, believed, and patiently waited for the miracle. Jesus confirmed it was his faith, his Believing Prayer, that had done it, and the soldier received just as he had believed:

Then Jesus said to the centurion, "Go your way;
and as you have believed, so let it be done for you."
And his servant was healed that same hour.
Matthew 8:13

Believing Prayer is also persistent; but rather than being persistent in asking, it is **persistent in believing.** It does not waver. It does not change. It does not tear down in doubt, what is built up in faith. It stands firm on the promises of God written in His holy Word and does not move, no matter what storms may come, no matter how grim or impossible the circumstances appear to be. It holds on to the promise and doesn't let go. Believing Prayer welcomes the impossible, because it is banking on a God who LOVES to do impossible things for His children.

When a situation moves from bad, to worse, to impossible, the faith which empowers Believing Prayer does not shrink or break down. In fact, it is strengthened even more. The bigger the problem, the more impossible the situation, the more glory goes to God. The Father delights in doing the impossible, because it strengthens the faith of His children and displays His splendor. In fact, if your prayers and requests, hopes and dreams are **not** nearing the realm of impossibility, chances are they are TOO SMALL!

Sometimes, the Father delays and intentionally holds back, so we will push past pint-sized prayers and dream bigger, impossible dreams, which become Believing Prayers.

Jesus intentionally delayed answering when He received word that Lazarus was sick. He waited and allowed death to take its natural course (John 11:6). It would have been easy for Him to say the word and heal Lazarus even from a distance, but He saw the opportunity for God to receive greater glory from an impossible situation. And He told the disciples He was glad for their sakes that Lazarus had died, because it would serve to strengthen their faith (John 11:15).

God the Father is still looking for opportunities in our lives to work greater wonders and receive greater glory in doing the impossible. And it's only impossible in our eyes, not His. He is the One who spoke the world into existence with a word from His mouth. From His perspective, it is no more difficult to heal a bruised knee than to raise the dead or to move a mountain. And it is *our faith* which moves Him to move that mountain.

There are four main elements to Believing Prayer: **Ask, Believe, Thank, and Receive.**

1) Believing Prayer <u>asks</u>. It brings the need before the Father, humbly asking Him to answer, to meet the present need in His way and His time.

2) Believing Prayer **believes**. Instead of festering and worrying if the need will be met or looking for another way to make it happen "just in case" God doesn't answer, it patiently waits for His plan to unfold and His way to appear. It knows He will answer in His time, and He doesn't need us to make a way for Him to work.

3) Believing Prayer **thanks**. A faithful heart is a grateful heart; it gives thanks and praise to the Father for meeting the need *even before the need is met*. It is completely confident the answer is coming; therefore, it is already thankful for it.

4) Believing Prayer **receives**. It stands ready to receive the provision from above *even before the answer arrives.* It is not taken by surprise, because it was expecting all along to receive from God exactly what was needed. It knows the answer is coming; therefore it prepares in advance to receive the answered prayer.

Jesus, whose prayers and faith are always flawless, modeled this for us to follow while He was here on earth. He multiplied the five loaves of bread and two fish to feed 5,000 people:

He said to the disciples, "Make them sit down in groups of fifty." And they did, and made them all sit down. Then He took the five loaves and the two fish, and looking up to heaven, He gave thanks and broke them, and gave them to the disciples to set before the multitude.
Luke 9:16

By lifting the small meal to heaven, Jesus brought the need to the Father, **asking** for provision, and **believing** God would hear and answer. Before the miracle even happened, He gave **thanks** to God. Jesus also prepared the disciples in advance to **receive** and distribute the provisions to the people by having them all sit down in groups of fifty. Thus, Jesus displayed: **Ask, Believe, Thank, Receive.**

Again, Jesus demonstrated these four elements when He raised Lazarus from the dead:

> *They took away the stone from the place where the*
> *dead man was lying. And Jesus lifted up His eyes and said,*
> *"Father, I thank You that You have heard Me.*
> *And I know that You always hear Me, but because of*
> *the people who are standing by I said this,*
> *that they may believe that You sent Me."*
> *Now when He had said these things He cried*
> *with a loud voice, "Lazarus, come forth!"*
> *And he who died came out...*
> John 11:41-44

Jesus presented His need when He lifted His eyes to Heaven, **asking** the Father to hear His prayer. He clearly **believed** God would hear and answer as He always does. He also **thanked** the Father in advance for hearing His prayer. Again, before the miracle even happened, Jesus was already prepared to **receive** Lazarus, because He told the people to remove the stone from the tomb. Here also, Jesus modeled: **Ask, Believe, Thank, Receive.**

The Greatest Giver

Believing Prayer is rooted in a powerful, merciful, scandalously generous, loving Father God.

The only reason anyone can pray in faith, believing God's promises, expecting good things from Him, is because of the character and nature of God: He is good. Supremely good.

What man is there among you who, if his son asks for bread, will give him a stone? Or if he asks for a fish, will give him a serpent? If you then, being evil, know how to give good gifts to your children, how much more will your Father who is in heaven give good things to those who ask Him!
Matthew 7:9-11

All people, even the very best people, will appear *evil* when placed in the light of the overwhelming goodness and generosity of God the Father in Heaven. Just as the flickering light from a candle is infinitely smaller than the radiance of the sun, so the magnanimity of man cannot even be compared to the scandalous generosity of God, the Greatest Giver. The dim light of the candle is lost in brilliant blinding light of the sun. Although minuscule in comparison, we give because God gives. And we were made to be like Him.

God is the Greatest Giver of all time.

This one simple truth forms the very foundation of our faith: "For God so loved the world that He **_gave_** ... (John 3:16). If God did not give, the enemy would have the eternal victory, our faith would be futile, and all would be lost. But **_God gave_** ... He gave the greatest gift He could possibly give when He gave us His one and only son, so we can experience eternal life through Him. And not only that, but He gave this great gift to us while we were still sinners and enemies of God! (Romans 5:8). If He was willing to give such a gift to His enemies, just imagine how incredibly good and generous He is to His own children, whom He adores!

In Christ alone, God has given us so much that Heaven can give no more! Yet, as if that wasn't enough, He still gives more! He gives breath and life, joy and laughter, love and family, friends and food, hearth and home, as well as all the infinite blessings of His incredible creation! Indeed, every good thing we have in our lives is directly from Him:

> *Every good gift and every perfect gift is from above,*
> *and comes down from the Father of lights, with*
> *whom there is no variation or shadow of turning.*
> James 1:17

The Bible challenges us: Because God has already given us the greatest gift of all in His Son, how could He possibly NOT also freely give us ALL things, if we would only ask Him (Romans 8:32)? **But we MUST ask in faith ...**

CHAPTER THREE

WHY FAITH?

*Without faith it is impossible to please God, for who-
ever comes to God must believe that He is, and that
He is a rewarder of those who diligently seek Him.*
Hebrews 11:6

It is genuine, heartfelt prayers born out of faith that
greatly please the Father. Whether our words are few or
many, when He sees our hearts sincerely seeking Him,
God is delighted. And He eagerly waits to reward those
who diligently seek His face.

*Let your prayers be without eloquence
rather than without faith.*

While serving God in Ghana, Africa with Mercy
Ships, a Christian medical ship, I came face to face with
the "faith of a child" in a small, five-year-old African boy.
Long ago, this very same childlike faith was pleasing to
Jesus as He walked the earth (Mark 10:13-16). The Lord

Jesus encouraged us to strive to have the heart of a child, so we may enter His Kingdom as children.

Jesus said, "of such is the Kingdom of God" (Matthew 19:14). To me, this little African child, in all his innocence and simplicity, possessed a great faith. He was the perfect example of sincere faith, without eloquent prayers, that pleased the Father's heart. This is his story.

A tall, dark, elegant, African Muslim woman came to the ship one day to receive medical care. She knew we were a Christian organization and that I was a Christian nurse. She pulled me aside during lunchtime and wanted to tell me about some "very disturbing behaviors" of her young son and ask my thoughts about the matter. She seemed distressed, so I agreed.

"Muslims hate Christians," She began. "My family knows this. My son knows this. Everyone knows this. Nevertheless, every Sunday morning, my five-year-old boy wakes up very early before the roosters, when everyone else is sleeping. He gets himself dressed, and he dresses his little sister, who is two years old. Then he sneaks out of the house, carrying his little sister with him on his back, and he walks two miles down the road to the nearest Christian church. Every Sunday, when he comes back, I beat him hard with a belt and tell him he must learn to hate all Christians! And every Sunday, he still goes, taking his little sister along. Even though I lock the doors, he still finds a way to escape. The people in the village make fun of me now, and say God is calling him to be a Christian preacher, but we are Muslims! I know you are all Christians. I wanted to come here and see what this Christian God is all about."

I answered her, "This is what you don't understand. While it is true that 'Muslims hate Christians,' what is even more true is this: Christians LOVE Muslims! And love is always stronger than hate. So, you cannot win. The Christian God is the God of love. He loves you and your son. And He is calling your whole family to Himself."

I had heard about the aggressive anti-Christian attitudes of the local Muslims in that region, so her violent behavior didn't shock me. What did shock me, and brought tears to my eyes, was the beautiful, simple, steadfast faith of a little five-year-old boy who knew every Sunday that he would come home to a beating, but still he returned again and again. When I talked to him, he smiled at me, but didn't speak much. This little boy's simple, silent faith spoke volumes to God—because the Heavenly Father always hears the deepest thoughts and most intimate motives hidden in the hearts of men—even in the heart of a child.

The simple faith of this small child moved the mighty heart of God, and eventually melted the hardened heart of his Muslim mother. I never saw this mother and child again, but when she left the ship, she did not leave the same. Her heart and her countenance were softened toward Christians and toward her son; transformed by faith and love. The faith was evident in her own child, and love was expressed by God's children—faithfully loving and serving the poor on the Mercy Ships.

Prayer with Faith

Just as faith without works is dead, so prayer without faith is also dead.

Faith is the elusive prize. It is the golden ticket. It is the reason we hope, the reason we pray, and the power behind our prayers. It is what God is searching for in the hearts of His children. Faith is the foundation of prayer. Without faith in a wonderfully good, merciful, generous, loving Father God, we have no one to hear our prayers and no reason to pray at all. It is **prayer with faith**, not prayer alone, that pleases God.

Not all prayers are pleasing to the Father.

Prayers devoid of all faith and heart are not worth the breath that forms them. The absence of faith is a serious grievance. For "whatever is not done in faith is sin" (Romans 14:23). In fact, the Bible tells us that the prayers and sacrifices of the ungodly are detestable to Him (Proverbs 15:8). But He delights in the faithful prayers of the upright. It also tells us that the man who prays without faith should not expect to receive ANYTHING from the Lord:

Let him ask in faith, with no doubting, for he who doubts is like a wave of the sea driven and tossed by the wind. For let not that man suppose that he will receive anything from the Lord.

James 1:6-7

*Faith is the anchor in the storms of life that secures us to God,
the only Immovable Rock.*

When the storms of life arrive (and they will arrive),
faith in God is the anchor that will keep your ship from being
driven and tossed by the wind. Without faith, the endless
waves of fear and doubt, the winds of temptation, and the
darkness of deception will sink even the strongest ship into
a sea of despair. It was faith that allowed Peter to walk on
the water to Jesus in the stormy sea (Matthew 14:22-33). It is
faith that is the enemy of fear; it causes our fears to flee and
our doubts to disperse, so we can stand firm in confidence
in the Lord. It is faith that brings the supernatural calm into
the center of the storms of life. It is faith which ushers in the
peace that passes all understanding (Philippians 4:7). And it
is faith in the only One who stills the sea, the only Refuge in
the storm, the Prince of Peace, who always brings us peace.

*Now when He got into a boat, His disciples followed Him,
and suddenly a great tempest arose on the sea, so that the
boat was covered with the waves. But He was asleep.
Then His disciples came to Him and awoke Him, saying,
"Lord, save us! We are perishing!" But He said to them,
"Why are you fearful, O you of little faith?"
Then He arose and rebuked the winds and the sea,
and there was a great calm.*
Matthew 8:23-26

Why did they have no peace when they were riding
in the boat with the Prince of Peace? Why were they so full

of fear and so empty of faith? When they woke Him from His sleep, did they think He could not, or simply would not rescue them in their sinking ship? How many times do we do the same thing? We believe in God, but when crisis hits, we fear the worst scenario. It paralyzes us. Like the disciples, we run around the boat in a panic, looking for Jesus who can calm the sea, trying to find some way to wake Him from His deep slumber.

But we fail to remember that the Master of the Storm is also the Maker of the Storm. He knew the storm would come and He chose to go to sleep anyway. God allows the storms and trials to come into our lives to test and strengthen our faith (1 Peter 1:6-7), which is much more precious than gold. Nevertheless, in a whirlwind of confusion, fear, and doubt, we struggle to catch our breath and find our faith, which is the key to calming the storm, bringing the miracle, and producing peace.

Faith is the key that unlocks the miracles and mysteries of God.

Faith unlocks the miracle of salvation, allowing us to become Children of God by faith in Jesus Christ (Galatians 3:26). It is only through faith that we can even begin the Christian journey in the first place. But faith is not just the beginning, it is the entire journey! The journey begins in faith when we are born again; it continues as we grow in faith and our faith is tested; and it ends as we finish the race, having kept the faith, to receive the reward (1 Peter 1:4). Just as Abraham "believed God and it was counted to him as righteousness" (Genesis 15:6), so we also believe God and become sons and daughters of Abraham by faith. We are justified and sanctified by that faith (Galatians 3:8, Acts 26:18).

Faith also gives us the wisdom of God which allows us to understand deep mysteries by the power of the Holy Spirit, and see things we could not otherwise see, nor understand (James 1:5-6). These mysteries are revealed through our faith by the Holy Spirit, who "searches all things, even the deep things of God" (1 Corinthians 2:9-10). Faith gives us eyes to search out the secrets of God and understand the mysteries of the Kingdom. And it is faith that opens our eyes to see God everywhere: in all of His creation, living and moving and breathing—working in every little detail of our lives, bringing all things together perfectly for our good (Rom 8:28).

Only by faith in Christ are we enabled to do the works of Jesus (John 14:12) and witness the mighty miracles of God. Faith is so essential to doing the works of Jesus that even Jesus Himself was limited by unbelief: He "could do no mighty works" in His own hometown because of the lack of faith of the people living there (Mark 6:5-6). Without faith, the power of God was hindered. But with faith, we can move many mountains, and nothing will be impossible for us (Matthew 17:20-21). By faith, we receive all the promises of God written in His Holy Word, including the promise of the Holy Spirit (Galatians 3:14). We ask in faith. We believe in faith. We receive in faith. And God is pleased.

Faith is the vehicle for the journey from Asking Prayer to Believing Prayer. We begin the journey in Asking Prayer. We must have faith to believe in God in the first place. We believe enough to come to Him in prayer and ask. However, our prayers are rooted in hope rather than in faith. We *hope* God may be inclined to hear us; to do us good; and to answer our prayers. But we lack the blessed assurance which comes from *faith*. And we have no certainty that He will hear and answer and grant our requests in the best possible way. All the while, the mountain seems immovable and the answer appears impossible—so we continue to ask.

Then faith comes along. It carries us to a place called Believing Prayer. This is where we learn to ask in faith—believing and knowing without a doubt that He hears, He answers, and He gives. Because He will never withhold anything good from us (Psalm 84:11). We learn to believe and prepare to receive. Because of faith, we know this for certain: the only impossible thing for God is for Him to be anything but good. Anything the Father ever gives his children is always wonderfully good. Armed with this knowledge, Believing Prayer asks with great expectation and confidence that prayers will be answered and great good is coming from the Father.

Ye of Little Faith

I am humbled to say the very first miracle I ever witnessed completely took me by surprise. At that time,

I was just beginning my life as a missionary nurse. I didn't realize it then, but my faith was very small. In fact, it was so small that after the miracle took place, I had a hard time believing the healing had actually occurred! And I was the one who prayed for it!

Many years ago, I was serving God in the Dominican Republic on a Haitian sugar-cane plantation. The Haitian villagers were living in squalor and had no access to medical care. One day, a Haitian woman brought her young daughter to me with a filthy, festering burn on her side, about the size of a man's hand. The girl had tripped and fallen into a fire and was burned by the hot coals. In that culture (as well as many others I have seen) the women cook on the ground and when they are finished, they cover the hot coals with dirt. The children then run around the village and quite often unwittingly fall into these fire pits. I cleaned the wound with saline and dressed it with Neosporin and a clean bandage. I prayed with her and her mother for healing for the little girl's wound.

The very next day, the same woman returned. She brought the little girl with her who still had the bandage on. I took it off to inspect the wound. There was no wound. There was no burn, no scab, no scar. There was nothing but pale, pink, smooth, healthy skin where the wound had once been. It was as if months of healing had occurred in less than 24 hours! At first, I didn't believe it was possible. I told the woman this could not be the same girl she brought to me the day before. She insisted that it was, that she was the only child she had who had fallen into the fire.

The mother was pleased at the healing, but not nearly as surprised as I was. She simply smiled, thanked me, thanked God, and went on her way. Perhaps it was the mother's faith—and not the missionary's—that healed her daughter. Either way, I thank God that it doesn't take much faith at all to make a huge difference in someone's life.

Corporate Faith

Again, I say to you that if two of you agree on earth concerning anything that they ask, it will be done for them by My Father in heaven. For where two or three are gathered together in My name, I am there in the midst of them.
Matthew 18:19-20

Faith is a powerful force. Even a minuscule amount of it, a tiny mustard seed, can do amazing things. Faith can bring about huge changes in our world; especially when it is pooled together with the faith and prayers of other like-minded believers. There is tremendous untapped potential in the unified faith of a body of believers. Whole cities, governments, and countries have been transformed by the power of corporate faith and Believing Prayer. When a group of dedicated believers simply agree to come together in Believing Prayer and seek God, they have the power to change the world. There are so many examples of this, that it would require too many books to contain them. Just as

God is pleased with the faith of an individual, He is also greatly pleased with the united faith of the body of Christ.

There is a mysterious power that exists in unity—whether for good or for evil. When people are truly unified, it is astounding what can be accomplished. This has been evident since the early days of man. Long ago, before the great flood, and before people were scattered across the earth, the Bible says mankind was unified. They had one language, one heart, and one purpose together. They were building the tower of Babel (Genesis 11:1-4).

God came down to see what man was building. When He saw their unity and what they were accomplishing, this was His intriguing remark:

> *Indeed the people are one and they all have one language, and this is what they begin to do; now nothing that they propose to do will be withheld from them.*
>
> Genesis 11:6

This is when the Bible says God brought different languages into the world, to force man to scatter across the earth (Genesis 11:7-9). Surely the power of corporate faith in God combined with complete unity is an unstoppable force to be reckoned with. And "nothing they propose to do will be withheld from them..."

We know corporate faith is near and dear to the heart of Christ, because it was the theme of His farewell discourse the night He was betrayed, shortly before He died. He prayed for all the believers who would ever live—that they would have unity in their faith in Him:

*...that they all may be one, as You, Father, are in
Me, and I in You; that they also may be one in Us,
that the world may believe that You sent Me.*

John 17:21

Even though the Christian church on earth appears to
be disjointed, unity in love, corporate prayer, and a unified
faith are the final goals Jesus had in mind. Although we
don't see it now, we will certainly see it one day, because
Jesus prayed, and His prayers never go unanswered.

Faith and Miracles

Man looks at the miracle, but the Father looks at faith.

Of course, everyone loves to see miracles happen,
to watch a mountain move, to have prayers answered and
dreams come true. We know faith makes all of this happen.
Miracles, signs, wonders, and answered prayers bring God
praise, honor, and glory. They are an important part of the
redemption story. They also serve to strengthen our faith
as well as the faith of others. But that begs the question:
Which is greater, faith or the miracle?

*It is faith that brings the miracle. But the miracle—no matter
how great—is only temporary.*

The crippled man's legs will eventually wear out. The woman who escaped death will eventually die. Lazarus' body was raised from the dead. He came out of the tomb into the light of day, only to return once more to death and the grave. Moses performed a tremendous miracle when he parted the Red Sea (Exodus 14). Nevertheless, it soon returned to its natural state, just as if nothing had happened. And there it remains to this day, under the rule of nature. The laws of nature in all creation were created by God, and so they can also be suspended by God whenever He wills. However, they still rule our world today.

Thus, every physical miracle and every answer to earthly prayers is only just for a little while, because nature inevitably takes over and runs its course. The miracle fades, the mountain sinks into the sea, the money gets spent, the answered prayer becomes a memory, or perhaps a testimony—and it is *faith* that remains. It is only faith and the memory of the miracles that we will take with us when we go.

The real prize, the greatest treasure is not the miracle. It is our faith.

Faith is powerful, prolific, and pleasing to God, but never passive. It cannot afford to be passive because it is not alone in this world. Faith has an enemy. There are many forces fighting against faith. And the enemy would like nothing more than to see our faith permanently shipwrecked on the shore. Strong faith is not for the faint of heart. It does not come without a struggle. Just as Abraham's faith required him to sacrifice Isaac (Genesis 22), so our faith—if it is genuine—will also require sacrifice. Faith does not quietly coast along without ever encountering a battle. Just to survive, *faith must fight.*

CHAPTER FOUR

FAITH FIGHTS

*Fight the good fight of faith, lay hold on eternal life,
to which you were also called and have confessed the
good confession in the presence of many witnesses.*
I Timothy 6:12

In the summer of 2014, while serving in Honduras with Health Teams International, I met Katherine, a Honduran believer, who was working with us as a medical translator. I didn't realize it then, but God had a special calling on her life. *Katherine was a Faith Fighter.*

Born into a well-to-do Honduran family in Tegucigalpa, the capital of Honduras, Katherine had far more opportunities to succeed than most women in her country. She was educated in the finest schools, connected to all the right people, highly intelligent, drop-dead gorgeous, and—as if that wasn't enough—she was also incredibly kind. She could have easily become a doctor or a lawyer or anything she wanted. She chose a different path.

Katherine had only been a born-again believer for about a year when I met her, but her passion for God was contagious. After serving the poor in her country with our team, her heart was wide open to God. She told Him she would dedicate her life to serving the poor. God heard that prayer. Not long after that, Katherine joined an outreach with her church to visit the trash dump in Tegucigalpa. What she saw that day changed her life forever: huge mountains of filthy, foul smelling trash for miles and miles; and on top of those mountains—mingling with the buzzards, rats, and dogs—were thousands of families! Men, women, and children of all ages meandering through the filth, most of them barefoot!! They were climbing up and down the monstrous piles of waste looking for recyclable items to sell and discarded food to eat.

Instead of responding in disgust or despair, *she chose to fight*: to fight injustice, hopelessness, and poverty; to fight for those who could not fight for themselves. Katherine Mejia had found her calling. She became a Faith Fighter.

These outcasts of society had literally lived off the trash mountain for generations, and they were barely surviving with no basic medical care, no education, and no hope of ever getting out—until God tapped young Katherine on the shoulder, and she responded with a resounding "Yes!"

In a few short years, with the help of her great God, her wise friend Pastor Jeony, and many generous, compassionate hearts, Katherine founded "Grace Honduras," a ministry to the people of the dump. It now offers an education for their children (kindergarten all the way through university), basic medical care, clean water, food, a seminary, and empowerment programs to teach women marketable skills. Now, the destiny of an entire community is radically changed, and all because one young woman, a Faith Fighter, decided to use her faith in God to fight poverty—and won. [1]

Where the Battle is Won

Whenever Moses held up his hand, Israel prevailed, and whenever he lowered his hand, Amalek prevailed.
Exodus 17:11

After the triumphal exit from Egypt, the Israelites were journeying towards the promised land with Moses, their fearless leader. They were suddenly attacked by Amalek and his warriors. Moses sent Joshua and his men down into the valley to do battle with Amalek. Meanwhile, Moses went up on the mountain to do battle in faith and prayer. He raised his hands in prayer over the battle down below. Whenever Moses lowered his hands, Joshua would lose, so Moses kept his hands held high. Eventually, when he grew tired, Aaron and Hur helped to secure the victory by holding Moses' hands up until Amalek's army was finally defeated by Joshua and his mighty men.

The battle was fought in the valley by the sword, but it was won on the mountain by faith.

Jesus battled in faith and prayer the night before his arrest. In a peaceful, quiet garden, where He sweat drops of blood, our Lord faced the horrific decision to surrender to God's will and accept crucifixion on a Roman cross. By the time His hour had come, Jesus was ready. His decision was made, and the outcome was determined. He had already fought and won the battle of faith and obedience with four small words: "Thy will be done" (Luke 22:42).

The victory of the cross of Christ was decided the night before in the garden of Gethsemane.

When times of trials and temptations arise, if we have not already built up our own faith—whether on the mountain, in the garden, or in our own private prayer closets—then we may lose the battle. But if we continually seek the Lord in prayer and faith before the struggle even occurs, we can rest assured that God will fight our battles, and we need only to be still (Exodus 14:14).

Many people turn to God when life takes a turn for the worse. But times of trials and testing are not the ideal times to learn how to pray. When a crisis hits, we do not always "rise to the occasion." Too often, we fall to the level of our faith, just as Simon Peter did when Jesus was arrested. Even though he was warned, he still denied Christ three times:

And the Lord said, "Simon, Simon! Indeed, Satan
has asked for you, that he may sift you as wheat,
but I have prayed for you, that your faith should not fail;

and when you have returned to Me, strengthen your
brethren." But he said to Him, "Lord, I am ready to go
with You, both to prison and to death." Then He said,
"I tell you, Peter, the rooster shall not crow this day
before you will deny three times that you know Me."

Luke 22:31-32

I'm not sure what Peter felt when he heard the news: he was going to be handed over to Satan to be "sifted like wheat." I wouldn't imagine he was thrilled with the idea, but it wasn't his plan after all—it was God's. It's clear he didn't believe he could ever deny Christ. He thought his faith was too strong for that. However, we are told the purpose of this trial was for his faith, that it "should not fail," and after the trial was over, he would return (presumably with a stronger faith) so he could strengthen his brethren. And that's exactly what happened. The trial indeed served to strengthen his faith. Peter did return, just as Jesus claimed he would. And Peter did follow Jesus both to prison and to his own death on a cross, just as Peter claimed he would (John 21:18-19).

The Armor of God

Put on the whole armor of God, that you may be
able to stand against the wiles of the devil. For we
do not wrestle against flesh and blood, but against
principalities, against powers, against the rulers of the
darkness of this age, against spiritual hosts of wickedness

in the heavenly places, Therefore, take up the whole
armor of God, that you may be able to withstand
in the evil day, and having done all, to stand.
Ephesians 6:11-13

Young David was told to wear the king's armor when he was going against Goliath to fight the king's battle (1 Sam 17:38). David, another Faith Fighter, believed God and had faith to fight when no one else did. Like David, we are also told to put on the King's armor, *The Armor of God*, and become Faith Fighters. However, we fight "not against flesh and blood" like the giant Goliath, but against bigger, more powerful, more destructive giants: against the "rulers of the darkness of this age." These rulers of darkness, these "spiritual forces of wickedness," are fought by faith with prayer and praise. And most often, the battlefield is in the heart and in the mind, because they attack the hearts and the minds of people. The enemy, the god of this world, lures the hearts and blinds the minds of men to keep them locked in confusion, sin, and disbelief (2 Corinthians 4:4). Faith Fighters fight to set them free.

Katherine, the Honduran Faith Fighter, encountered this bondage in her work with the people of the trash dump. Even now, while their basic needs are met—they receive food and shelter and their children are enrolled in the Christian school—these people still suffer terribly in their hearts and in their minds. They are trapped in deep psychological and emotional cages that stem from living and working in a huge garbage pile every day of their lives with no hope in sight. They believe they are as worthless as the garbage they collect. Christ came to love them and set them free. He calls us to do the same: to be set free; to set others free; to advance the Kingdom of God against the enemy and to obtain the victory.

Victory is Our Destiny

For whatever is born of God overcomes the world. And this is the victory that has overcome the world—our faith.
1 John 5:4

Victory is not just a nice idea or a pipe dream. ***Victory is our destiny.*** We are promised by God that victory in the battle is ***already*** ours because the war has already been won in the birth, death, and resurrection of Jesus Christ. He trampled Satan, abolished death, and brought life and immortality to light through the gospel (2 Tim 1:10). He already won the victory for us. Victory belongs to the children of God. It is rightfully ours. All we need to do is take it.

After World War II was won and Hitler's army was defeated, the war was officially over. However, the Allied forces spent many months (and lost many lives in the process) advancing through enemy occupied territory, setting free the captured cities, and actualizing the victory that had already been secured for them.

On May 7, 1945, Nazi Germany surrendered. The German High Command sat with the Allies and signed a document of unconditional surrender of all German military forces, effective immediately. The American foot soldiers never saw that document; they only heard the good news from their beloved General George Patton—and they believed what they heard.

After hearing that the war was over, the American soldiers did not go directly home. On behalf of the Allied armies, they carried on, with the full power and authority of the American flag behind them. They continued to advance into every town, driving out the remaining enemy armies who were already defeated.

In a similar way, Faith Fighters and all believers are foot soldiers of God. We are called to advance into enemy territory, to drive out the forces of darkness that have already been defeated. Much like the brave American soldiers who received word from their leaders that the war was over, we also hear and believe the Good Word delivered to us by our Captain—that the enemy has officially been defeated and the war has been won. Jesus Christ Himself gave full authority to the disciples (which we also have if we choose to follow Christ). He gave them (and us) authority over the enemy: to conquer the enemy, to drive out impure spirits, to bring righteousness and truth, and to heal sickness and disease (Matthew 10:1).

Armed with this knowledge, we advance with the full authority of victors, under the banner of the cross of Christ. If we do not fully comprehend and believe that our King has already defeated the foe, then we will lack the power and authority to command the enemy to stand down. When we fight by faith with prayer and praise, standing on the authority of God's word, the enemy has no choice but to flee.

Because of the great love and sacrifice of Jesus Christ, no matter what the circumstances appear to be, or just how bad things look, we are always victorious, because He obtained the victory for us:

Who shall separate us from the love of Christ?
Shall tribulation, or distress, or persecution, or famine, or
nakedness, or peril, or sword? As it is written: "For Your sake
we are killed all day long; We are accounted as sheep for the
slaughter." Yet in ALL these things we are MORE than
conquerors through Him who loved us.
Romans 8:35-37

Why Fight?

The purpose of Believing Prayer and Fighting Faith is
essentially the Lord's Prayer—to bring the Kingdom of the
King of Kings.

Our Father in heaven, hallowed be Your name. Your king-
dom come, Your will be done on earth as it is in heaven . . .
Matthew 6:9-10

We are called to fight the good fight of faith, to advance the Kingdom of God and the will of God in heaven (and everything that comes with it) onto the whole earth. In the Kingdom of God there is no sickness or disease, poverty or greed, lust or lies; nor selfishness, violence, pride, jealousy, murder, or worthlessness—the list goes on and on. Just as things are in heaven, so we pray they may also be on earth. Faith fights every day to see that happen. As children of light, we are called to make war against the darkness, to usher in God's Kingdom.

In bringing the Kingdom to earth, we are preparing for the final return of the King.

Furthermore, we are promised by God: that He will be with us in the battle; that we will win the war; and that we will receive a crown—a reward in Heaven for a battle well fought, and a job well done. This is why faith fights.

Faith fights at the foot of a sickbed. Faith fights when a marriage is failing. Faith fights for the return of the prodigal sons and daughters. Faith fights to save the lost. Faith fights financial ruin. Faith fights poverty, racism, hatred and hopelessness. Faith fights injustice and abuse. Faith fights to set the prisoners free. Faith fights depression, addiction, and temptation. Faith fights for those who cannot fight for themselves. Faith fights confusion, disillusionment, fear and doubt. Faith fights and fights and fights and never, ever gives up.

Above all these things, faith fights against sin. Because it is sin that separates us (and all people) from God the Creator. It is sin that makes Him hide His face, so He cannot hear our prayers (Is 59:2). And it is sin that weakens our faith, so we cannot fight.

You have not yet resisted to bloodshed, striving against sin.
Hebrews 12:4

In Hebrews 11, the famous Faith Fighters did remarkable things through faith. They stood strong and believed without wavering until their faith became reality:

. . . who through faith subdued kingdoms, worked
righteousness, obtained promises, stopped the mouths of lions,
quenched the violence of fire, escaped the edge of the sword,
out of weakness were made strong, became valiant in battle,
turned to flight foreign armies. Women received their dead
raised to life again, others were tortured and did not accept
deliverance, that they might obtain a better resurrection."
Hebrews 11:33-35

All of these and many more great feats were accomplished through fighting faith. We are encouraged to follow in their footsteps. They were people just like us, with hang-ups and quirks; baggage and failures; doubts and fear (James 5:17). But, like Katherine, they chose to fight the good fight of faith, to war against the rulers of darkness— and they won! The very same faith that they had is still available for us today! But it cannot be manufactured. *It must be given . . .*

CHAPTER FIVE

THE GIFT OF FAITH

I indeed baptize you with water; but One mightier than
I is coming, whose sandal strap I am not worthy to loose,
He will baptize you with the Holy Spirit, and fire.
Luke 3:16

One cold Sunday morning at Cornerstone Nashville,[2] my home church in Nashville, Tennessee, I had an experience that changed everything for me. Our beloved pastors Galen and Maury Davis were out of the country at a pastor's conference, so they left us with a substitute pastor that weekend. His name was Glen Berteau. I don't remember a lot about what he said, except for the way he talked about the Holy Spirit. It made me hungry.

Having been raised as a good Baptist girl and a dedicated Christian since college, I knew all about it. I knew I already had the Holy Spirit. I had felt Him and seen Him work many times. He went with me to Africa, all over the world on mission trips, and accompanied me home. I loved Him. I knew Him well—or so I thought. In addition, our pastor, Galen Davis, often spoke about the Holy Spirit, the importance of being filled with the Spirit, and the gifts of the Spirit, which are available to all believers. However, I couldn't shake this nagging thought which eventually became a prayer: *Maybe there's more...*

That morning, Glen Berteau spoke again about the baptism of the Holy Spirit and believers being "filled" with the Spirit. He offered an altar call for anyone who wanted the Holy Spirit, either to be baptized or filled. I wasn't sure which one I needed, but I knew I wanted more. I didn't have anything to lose in asking, so I went. I knelt with my eyes closed in excitement and expectation, waiting for something amazing to happen. Nothing happened.

I went home empty-handed that day. But I wasn't worried. *God can do whatever He wants, whenever He wants. It's fine by me,* I reasoned.

The following evening, I was sitting alone in my cozy cabin in the woods, warming myself by the fire. As was my custom, I started to read the Bible and casually pray. I guess God decided that was as good a time as any to show up. I began to feel a deep inward hunger for God and a deep peace at the same time. Suddenly, I felt the presence of the Lord fall in the room and I fell to my knees. With tears streaming down my face, I was immediately filled with more joy, peace, warmth, happiness, and love than I ever thought was possible. I knew it was Him. I had known Him all along, but never like this. My heart was overwhelmed with awe, amazement, and adoration for God.

Instantly, my mind was so filled with thoughts of the Lord, there was no room for anything else—the fire, the cabin, my hot chocolate, my body face-down on the floor, the future, the past, my horses, my nice little comfortable life—in a moment, He consumed it all. All I could think about was Him. All I wanted to do was worship.

I wanted to speak, but I was speechless. I opened my mouth to praise the Lord, and I didn't understand the words that came out. Somehow, I knew God was perfecting His own praise from my imperfect lips. And the praise was coming from His own Spirit in my heart, straight to the heart of God. It was building my faith, so I just kept praising God. It lasted for several hours, and in many ways, it has never stopped.

For weeks after that night, I sought the Lord with all my might. I searched the Scripture for words about being filled with the Holy Spirit, speaking in tongues, dreams and visions, spiritual gifts, and everything I was experiencing. I learned about the "gift of faith" along with the other gifts listed in the Bible (1 Corinthians 12:1-11).

Because it was Christmastime, and I had a few presents under my tree, I thought it might be appropriate to make a wish list for God. I decided to ask Him for a gift. After looking at the long list, I figured faith was a pretty good place to start. So, I asked the Holy Spirit for the gift of faith, not knowing what to expect. And as a result, this little book was born.

For by grace you have been saved through faith,
and that not of yourselves; it is the gift of God.
Ephesians 2:8

Faith is not from man. It is from God (Romans 10:17). It is always a gift from God which we can gratefully receive and freely give back to Him. All faith, even saving faith, is a gift from God. Just as every perfect gift is always from Him (James 1:17), so the perfect gift of faith comes down from the Father of Lights. We only have faith because He gives us faith. There is no other way to get it. It cannot be manufactured by man (Ephesians 2:9).

However, the *gift of faith* is a unique, separate gift of the Holy Spirit. This is not referring to *saving faith* that a person must have to trust in Christ and receive salvation. The Bible says this gift is given after salvation and the baptism of the Holy Spirit (1 Corinthians 12:9). It is given by the Holy Spirit to believers who ask for it (1 Corinthians 12:31). Just like any other gift, it must be received. The gift of faith is received by faith.

We ask in faith. We believe in faith. We receive in faith.

The gift of faith helps believers build up their faith to move mountains, and it makes Believing Prayer possible. It is essential in spreading the gospel, doing the works of the Kingdom, resisting the fear of man, pushing back the powers of darkness, and bringing God's Kingdom to earth. All the gifts of the Spirit require some measure of faith (Romans 12:3).

Faith is the foundation and the bedrock
on which everything else relies.

The Rainstorm

When the Holy Spirit and tongues of fire first fell on the apostles and the new believers in the first century church in Jerusalem, there was much bewilderment about what was happening. Jesus had told the apostles to wait in Jerusalem for the Holy Spirit, who had not yet come into the world (Acts 1:4). They waited, He came, and the fire fell (Acts 1 & 2). In all the excitement, Peter stood up with the other eleven apostles to clear the air and confirmed that this was the fulfillment of the prophecy written long ago, by the prophet Joel:

> *And it shall come to pass in the last days, says God, that I will pour out of My Spirit on all flesh; your sons and your daughters shall prophesy, your young men shall see visions, your old men shall dream dreams, and on my menservants and on my maidservants I will pour out My Spirit in those days; and they shall prophesy.*
>
> Acts 2:17-18

This prophecy in Joel is referred to as the "latter rain" of the Spirit of God (Joel 2:23). We are still living in the "last days" of the latter rain. God is still pouring out His Spirit on all His children equally: in every culture, in every race, men and women, old and young, rich and poor. We are living in the days of the Great Rainstorm! Right now, He is pouring out His Spirit; blessings and fruit; new wine, grain and oil; victory, peace and prosperity; power, prophecy, dreams, visions, the gift of faith, and all the gifts of the Spirit (Joel 2:19-29).

Not long after the Holy Spirit fell on the apostles in Jerusalem, God began pouring out His Spirit on all believers: male and female, Jew and Gentile (Acts 2:38-39). The Jewish believers who followed Peter were astonished "because the gift of the Holy Spirit had been poured out on the Gentiles also, for they heard them speak with tongues and magnify God" (Acts 10:45-46). When the apostles received God's Spirit, they were filled with faith and boldness.

For I will pour water on him who is thirsty, and floods on the dry ground; I will pour My Spirit on your descendants, and My blessing on your offspring.
Isaiah 44:3

Just as rain falls on everyone without discrimination, the "latter rain" of God's spirit and blessings, including the gift of faith, is also for everyone. It is poured out on "him who is thirsty." If that's true, then why doesn't every thirsty soul experience God's rain? Why isn't everyone soaked with His wonderful blessings? And who can stand in the middle of a rain shower and never get wet?

Whoever holds an umbrella.

It is *faith* that allows us to enter the Kingdom; to thirst for God's Spirit; to trust in His goodness—so much so, that we are compelled to drop our umbrellas; to leave our dry, comfortable shelters; and run out into the pouring rain—

only to find ourselves happily drenched in the abundant blessings, love, mercies, presence, and gifts of the Spirit of God. We don't need to wait. We don't need to pray for rain. Because, God is not waiting to pour out His Spirit. It's already raining...

And it shall come to pass in that day that the mountains shall drip with new wine, the hills shall flow with milk, and all the brooks of Judah shall be flooded with water; a fountain shall flow from the house of the Lord and water the valley.
Joel 3:18

The Gift Reflects the Giver

In my travels around the world, serving the poor, I have received different kinds of gifts from different kinds of people: a doll from a young Russian girl; plantains in Africa; Chiclets from children in Mexico; yak milk from shepherds in Tibet; backyard coffee beans from farmers in Honduras; a headless chicken in Nepal; a beautiful longyi skirt from a woman in Myanmar; handmade wool socks from an old man in a cave in Turkey; a free trip to a horse farm in Inner Mongolia from a wealthy Chinese businessman; and a priceless oil painting from a world renowned artist in Beijing.

In every instance, each gift revealed the same generous, kind, loving heart of the giver. But each gift was different and reflected the individual giver in unique ways—where they live, what they value, their status in life, their personal resources, and their ability to give good gifts.

Each gift is a direct reflection of the giver. Every giver, out of the goodness of his or her heart, gave what was valuable and important in their eyes. They expected their gift to be received with gratitude and used for its own unique purpose, not to be discarded or misused. This is true of people and it is also true of God.

> *If you then, being evil, know how to give good gifts to your children, how much more will your heavenly Father give the Holy Spirit to those who ask Him?*
> Luke 11:13

Our Heavenly Father loves us so much that He already gave us the ultimate gift in sacrificing His son, so we could be adopted into His eternal family. If everything He does is perfect, wouldn't it also be true that everything He *gives* is perfect? Why then, would any of His other gifts not be comparable to the greatest, most infinitely perfect gift of Jesus Christ??

The Greatest Giver cannot give anything but the greatest gifts.

After the gift of His son, the next thing He could give us is the Holy Spirit. And that's exactly what He did. In this verse, Jesus specified that the Father gives the Holy Spirit "to those who ask Him." We are instructed to ask for the Holy Spirit and to earnestly desire and pursue the gifts of His Spirit for the building up of the body and the works of the Kingdom (1 Corinthians 12:31, 1 Corinthians 14:1). It is only the Spirit of God who gives the gift of faith.

God knew from the very beginning we would need the Holy Spirit, but that wasn't enough. ***He wants us to know we need the Holy Spirit.*** We need God's Spirit to impart faith into our hearts. That's why He wants us to seek Him; to ask for Him. That's why He allows us to hunger for Him, so we can recognize and realize our incredibly deep need of Him. And that's why He wants us to "earnestly desire and pursue" the Holy Spirit along with the gifts He gives, lest we should take Him for granted and discard or misuse His gifts.

The gift of faith is only one of nine listed spiritual gifts, but it is essential. It is what empowers believers to do the works of Jesus, which we are all supposed to be imitating. Jesus gave us an example of the kind of faith He wanted His followers to have:

> *Now in the morning, as He returned to the city, He was hungry. And seeing a fig tree by the road, He came to it and found nothing on it but leaves and said to it, "Let no fruit grow on you ever again." Immediately the fig tree withered away. And when the disciples saw it, they marveled, saying, "How did the fig tree wither away so soon?" So Jesus answered and said to them, "Assuredly, I say to you, if you have faith and do not doubt, you will not only do what was done to the fig tree, but also if you say to this mountain, 'Be removed and be cast into the sea,' it will be done. And whatever things you ask in prayer, believing, you will receive."*
>
> Matthew 21:18-22

It is Believing Prayer filled with faith that can cause the fig tree to wither or the mountain to be removed and cast into the sea. This faith which is free from doubt is the faith Jesus was looking for in His followers. It is faith that comes from the Father.

Blessed to Be a Blessing

All the gifts of the Holy Spirit, including the gift of faith, are meant to be exercised, poured out, and used up for the glory of the Kingdom of God. They were never meant to be abused, hidden or hoarded. The gifts were always meant to be given away for the building up of the body. Just as He pours out on us; we also should pour out on others. Each gift is given by the Holy Spirit individually as He wills (1 Corinthians 12:11). The gifts are all different and unique in their functions, but the primary purpose is the same: for the "profit of all" (1 Corinthians 12:7, 1 Corinthians 14:12)—not for the profit of one.

This truth goes back to the very foundation of our faith. Abraham was blessed by God, so he in turn, would be a blessing to the whole world (Genesis 12:2). The blessing of God was never just for Abraham alone. God promised Abraham that through him all the families of the earth would receive a blessing (Genesis 12:3). That promise is still being fulfilled today. God is a god of multiplication, generosity, and abundance. He wants us to be the same way. He intends for us to pour out the blessings and use the gifts we receive from Him with outrageous generosity. This generosity enlarges our hearts, and makes room for Him to give us even more:

Give, and it will be given to you; good measure, pressed down, shaken together, and running over will be put into your bosom.
Luke 6:38

Without pouring out, we become stagnant and self-serving. A stagnant body of water can be a major hazard. It quickly becomes a breeding ground for parasites, bacteria, and disease. In order to remain healthy, water must flow. In the same way, the blessings and gifts we receive must flow out. When we are showered with the blessings of God's Spirit, we must pour out what we receive: our lives, our talents, our gifts, our love, our finances, our time. Sometimes, we may become selfish. We may be tempted to hoard the gifts and blessings for ourselves. This is when the blessing becomes a curse.

We Ask Amiss

When we ask for something, and we have selfish, wrong, or sinful motives, we will not receive what we are asking for because God sees our hearts and how we would misuse the gift He gives (James 4:3). When we come to seek the Lord or ask something of Him, our hearts should be clean and right with God the Father, and also with our fellow man (Psalm 66:18, Matthew 5:23-24). The Holy

Spirit and the gifts of the Spirit are for those who walk humbly with God in obedience, with clean hands and pure hearts (Acts 5:32, Psalm 24:3-4). When we ask in pride and selfishness or with wrong motives, we will not receive:

> *You lust and do not have. You murder and covet and cannot obtain. You fight and war. Yet you do not have because you do not ask. You ask and you do not receive, because you ask amiss, that you may spend in on your pleasures.*
> James 4:3

Exercising the Gifts

> *A man's gift makes room for him and brings him before great men.*
> Proverbs 18:16

When we do pour out what we receive, we are exercising the gifts He's given. We are learning how to use them effectively. The Bible instructs us to use our individual gifts according to the measure of grace and faith we have been given (Romans 12:6-8). Without action and exercise of any gift, we will not improve, regardless of the measure of faith.

Just because a man is born with a natural talent or gift, doesn't mean he will automatically be successful in performing that task without ever practicing or putting in any effort. However, if a man does decide he wants to excel at something, he puts his whole heart into it and does everything he possibly can to improve his God-given talent. He strives to become the very best he can be in his chosen field. After he does this, doors will open for him that do not open for others. He will be taken to a higher level, to stand before kings and great men, because his faith and his gift were combined with action.

Do you see a man who excels in his work? He will stand before kings. He will not stand before unknown men.
Proverbs 22:29

CHAPTER SIX

FAITH TAKES ACTION

Faith is the substance of things hoped for and the evidence of things not seen.
Hebrews 11:1

A few years back, it was Christmastime in Nashville, Tennessee. My friends came over and asked if I wanted to plan a party to celebrate my birthday (which is in December) and Christmas as well. I had just been reading in Luke 14:12-14, where Jesus says, "When you give a party, a dinner, or a banquet, don't invite your friends, brothers, relatives, or rich neighbors, lest they repay you by inviting you back. Instead, invite the poor, the maimed, the lame, and the blind, and you will be blessed because they can't repay you. You will be repaid at the resurrection of the just."

I told my friends about this verse and that I wanted to put some action to my faith in God's Word—to *actually do* what Jesus suggested. Fortunately for me, they loved this idea. We decided to throw a big Christmas party for the homeless in downtown Nashville. We got permission to use our church ministry building and spread the word to the homeless people connected to the church ministry; apparently, word travels fast in the homeless community. We had little money between us, so we were depending on donations—and depending on God.

As soon as we stepped out in faith and obedience to follow His word, He showed up! With little time to prepare, no advertising, and only word of mouth to spread the news, surprisingly, donations came quickly: coffee from Starbucks; cakes, pies, and cookies from a local bakery; turkeys, vegetables, and sides from the grocery. Our little Christmas party for about 100 homeless people was turning into a great feast.

The only things missing were gifts. While sitting with my friend Stephanie, we began brainstorming ways to provide 100 tiny gifts for them. We read the verse in Luke 3:11 where Jesus says, "whoever has two coats, let him give to him who has none…" I went and looked in my closet; I had four coats, but even if I gave three of them away, we would still be short 97 coats! This wouldn't work. But we liked the idea, so we told God we needed 97 coats—or just however many He could spare.

About two days later, we received a random call from a woman whom none of us knew. She had heard through the grapevine what we were doing and contacted our church to find us. She said she had been collecting coats all year long for the homeless, and she would like to give us 300 coats for the Christmas party! God is a god of abundance—that was more than enough. It was a wonderful, memorable party for everyone involved. Our simple *faith combined with action* produced great results and eternal rewards.

True faith is always accompanied by some form of action.

James teaches that if a person is destitute and has no food and you tell him "Go in peace. Be warm and filled!" but you do nothing to meet his needs, then your words are void and useless. It is the same way with faith. If faith is not followed by action, then it is dead. Abraham's faith was only justified and made perfect because it was joined with his actions. His faith was working together with his works (James 2:15-22).

If a person proclaims he believes something, but it doesn't have any effect whatsoever on any of his outward actions, then there are only two possible options for that person: He is either deceiving others, or he is deceiving himself. Faith is the evidence of things unseen. Actions are the evidence of faith.

Faith without works is a lie.

Paralytic on the Roof

Then, behold, men brought on a bed a man who was paralyzed, whom they sought to bring in and lay before Him. And when they could not find how they could bring him in because of the crowd, they went up on the housetop

and let him down with his bed through the tiling into the
midst before Jesus. When He saw their faith,
He said to him, "Man, your sins are forgiven you."
Luke 5:18-20

When Jesus looked up and saw a crippled man being lowered from the ceiling by his friends, He knew they had faith enough to risk climbing on top of a house with a lame man! Their actions made it clear they had faith. They would never have gone to such extremes without extreme faith in Jesus' ability to heal the paralyzed man. Their faith in Jesus combined with love for their friend, moved them into action. And Jesus was moved when He saw their faith displayed by their actions. Virtually everyone who came to Jesus in the Bible displayed faith in some way by their actions, even if it was merely having enough faith to come and ask. True faith will always be accompanied by action.

Faith Walks

For we walk by faith, not by sight.
2 Corinthians 5:7

In my adventures with the Lord, I found myself one summer day, hiking in one of the largest mountain ranges in the world—Nepal. We had traveled as far as the road could take us; now we were hiking the rest of the way. It was a six-hour hike to reach the village where we were going to serve. We followed the trail up and down through picturesque peaks. As we rounded a bend, I looked up to see where it was going. When I scanned the horizon, I began to be concerned.

The path seemed to vanish right before our eyes. The entire face of the next mountain was nothing but steep, sheer rock, apparently the result of a gigantic landslide. From where I was standing, there was no safe way through this peak, only loose gravel covering slick rocks that led to massive cliffs. And those cliffs would surely deliver a swift death to anyone who slipped.

I began nervously questioning our guide whether this was the best and safest way to travel. He laughed and replied, "It's the only way!" He assured me there was a safe, solid path, but it was narrow and hidden. "The path is there! I promise. You just can't see it!" He called out as I followed behind. I decided to trust him and keep on walking, because he had walked this way many times before. I took the time to make sure my heart was right with God, just in case I would see Him face to face that day.

When we finally arrived at the entrance to the landslide mountain, just as he said, there was a small but solid footpath that led safely to the other side. But this path could not be seen from a distance. It was hidden in the landslide rocks. You could only see it when you were ready to walk on it.

This is often the case with faith. Sometimes the way is unsettling and seems unclear in the distance. The best course of action may not actually appear until we are ready to enter in. But the path is there. You just can't see it. So, we learn to trust the Guide who always knows the way; and step by step, we continue to walk by faith until the right road rises up to meet us. And then we find the narrow path leading safely to the other side of the mountain.

Elijah Takes Action

Elijah was a man with a nature like ours, and he prayed earnestly that it would not rain; and it did not rain on the land for three years and six months. And he prayed again, and the heaven gave rain, and the earth produced its fruit.
James 5:17-18

Elijah, another man who prayed for rain long ago, also displayed powerful faith in action. He had just won a great victory on Mt. Carmel against the prophets of Baal, and the fire of God had fallen and consumed the sacrifice (1 Kings18). There had been a drought for three years in the land. Before there was ever any sign of rain, and even before he prayed, Elijah told King Ahab to go eat and drink because he heard "the sound of abundance of rain" (1 Kings 18:41). He then bowed down to pray and commanded his servant to go up the mountain and look to the sea seven times. Each time, the servant saw no sign of rain, except the very last time. Elijah's servant saw a cloud "as small as a man's hand." That was all the evidence he needed. Elijah told the king to prepare the chariot to race down the mountain before the storm hit, and he himself raced down the mountain on foot before the king to the entrance of the city (1 Kings 18:41-46).

It was Elijah's faith in his God that spurred him into action. His actions were not based on present reality but on future faith. He saw and heard the rainstorm by faith before it ever occurred in reality. It's important to realize that while Elijah did act in faith, he didn't act in his own strength. The Bible says that "the hand of the Lord came upon him" and he outran Ahab's horse down the mountain (1 Kings 18:46). That was impossible for him to do in his own strength. When we walk with God, and we step out in faith to take action, we often find His hand upon us and we are no longer acting in our own strength. We are acting in His.

Actions done in faith out of love for God are always backed by the strength and power of His Holy Spirit.

When we act in faith, out of a sincere heart of love for God, we can never go wrong—even when the outcome is not what we were expecting. Faith in action always bears rich, abundant fruit in the Kingdom of God. And just like Elijah running down the mountain, when we fall short in the weakness and natural limitations of our own humanity, the Holy Spirit lifts our feet and empowers us. He allows us to do in His strength what we cannot do in our own strength. That's when we discover we truly can "mount up with wings like eagles, run and not grow weary, walk and not faint" (Isaiah 40:31).

Not by might nor by power, but by My Spirit,
says the Lord of hosts.
Zechariah 4:6

We are called to believe God, to take action, to do the works of God, to step out in faith, and to walk by faith, believing that the right road will appear and rise up to meet us. But we were never called to do it in our own strength. The Bible says we can do anything through Jesus Christ who gives us His strength (Philippians 4:13), but without His strength, we can do nothing (John 15:5).

By relying completely on the power of His Holy Spirit, we can do things we would otherwise never be able to do. We can be strong in all the ways we are weak. Even more than that, we can celebrate our weaknesses and limitations because His strength is perfected in them (2 Corinthians 12:9). And all of this is done through faith in action.

Faith Acts in Obedience

If you abide in Me and My words abide in you,
you will ask what you desire, and it shall be done for you;
by this My Father is glorified, that you bear much fruit;
so you will be my disciples. As the Father loved Me,
I also have loved you; abide in My love. If you keep
My commandments, you will abide in My love,
just as I have kept My Father's commandments
and abide in His love.
John 15:7-10

Jesus made it clear there are certain stipulations for the promise "Ask and you shall receive." This promise is not carte blanche. And God is certainly not a genie in a bottle, at our beck and call, to grant our every passing wish and whim. In order to consistently apply this powerful promise in our lives, we must do three things He commands us to do:

Ask in faith.   Abide in love.   Act in obedience.

We must ask in faith. When we ask without faith, we are told we can expect to receive nothing; and it's impossible to please God without faith. Faith is the essential ingredient of Believing Prayer and necessary in receiving our requests.

We must abide in the love of Christ. Jesus says that if we are abiding in Him and His love, then we will bear much fruit and we can ask anything we want and be sure we will receive it. If we do not abide in Him, and walk in His love, we can do nothing (John 15:5).

We must act in obedience to God and to His Word. Jesus said the way we abide in His love is to obey His commandments. He also said that if we love Him, we will obey Him (John 14:5). And we will receive whatever we ask from Him, "because we keep His commandments and do those things that are pleasing in His sight" (1 John 3:22). But if we disregard His word and refuse to act in obedience, we will receive nothing.

Even though we have faith, if we ask or act out of disobedience or contrary to God's Word, then we are no longer abiding in love. We can be sure we will receive nothing from Him. Furthermore, the Holy Spirit is only given to those who obey (Acts 5:32).

An example of a believer who had plenty of faith but did not abide in love or act in obedience is Simon the Sorcerer (Acts 8). Simon was a famous magician in Samaria who converted to Christianity. He believed in Jesus. He was baptized. He followed the apostle Philip. Simon saw that the miracles and signs done by the apostles were greater than his own dark magic arts, and he was amazed. Meanwhile, the apostles sent Peter and John to Samaria to bring the Holy Spirit to the new believers. These Samarians had accepted Christ but had not yet received the Holy Spirit (Acts 8:16).

Simon saw the power demonstrated by the Spirit, and he wanted it. He wanted to have the same ability to lay hands on someone to receive the Spirit. Simon believed. He had believed in Jesus, been baptized, and left his practice of sorcery to follow Philip. He certainly believed in the power of the Holy Spirit. However, his heart was not right. Instead of humbly asking God for the gift of the Spirit, as we are instructed to do, Simon offered to buy the Holy Spirit's power from Peter with money. This was Peter's reply:

*Your money perish with you, because you thought
that the gift of God could be purchased with money!
You have neither part nor portion in this matter,
for your heart is not right in the sight of God.
Repent therefore of this your wickedness and pray God
if perhaps the thought of your heart may be forgiven you.
For I see that you are poisoned by
bitterness and bound by iniquity.*
Acts 8:20-21

You could say Simon was acting in faith when he tried to buy God's power. He never would have asked for it if he didn't believe it was real. He had faith in the power and faith in the works of the Spirit. He was not condemned for his faith. He was condemned because his heart was wicked, sinful, and disobedient. He was neither walking in love nor acting in obedience. Judging by his history, and Peter's sharp rebuke, one might surmise that Simon's heart was corrupted by lust for money. Perhaps he saw the Holy Spirit's power as a quick way to make a profit.

Tithing in Faith

The act of tithing, giving one tenth of one's income to the Lord, is also faith in action, as well as an act of obedience. We are trusting God will meet our needs and bless us abundantly as He promises in His word (Malachi 3:8-10). We give by faith. The Bible says we are cursed when we withhold from Him and blessed when we give. We freely give our tithes and offerings back to God in faith because we love and obey Him, and we believe His promises. We are directly following His command when we return our first fruits back to Him, who gave us everything we have in the first place. Tithing regularly grows our faith in God, who always provides abundantly; and it also helps to guard against greed.

Tithing is a command from God, not a suggestion. However, by mandating the tithe, God is not after our bank accounts, as some may think. He is after our hearts.

In commanding us to give, He is teaching us to be more like Him, the Greatest Giver of all time. And when we finally capture a tiny piece of His giant heart, we begin to see things differently. Rather than calculating how much we can get, we begin to dream about how much we can give! Then we realize the 10% tithe is paltry. It is not the final goal. The tithe is just the beginning. The greatest goal would be the "reverse tithe"—keeping 10% for ourselves, and giving the rest to God to bless and help others and to build His Kingdom.

Real faith takes some form of action. But how can faith act on something it cannot see? Unless blindness hinders us, most of the actions (and reactions) we have in the physical world are based on something we see. The actions of faith are also largely based on what it can see. But faith does not operate through physical eyes. Therefore, we need *eyes of faith . . .*

CHAPTER SEVEN

EYES OF FAITH

*We do not look at the things which are seen but at the
things which are not seen. For the things which are seen
are temporary, but the things which are not seen are eternal.*
2 Corinthians 4:18

Dr. David Yonggi Cho is the founder of the largest
Christian church in the world, Yoido Full Gospel Church in
South Korea. The church claims a membership of 830,000
people. It has had a profound impact on the entire country
of South Korea, as well as many other countries all over the
world. Dr. Cho made it his life's practice to fix his eyes on
the unseen dreams and visions for the future, rather than
on his present circumstances. He was always looking to the
promises of God through eyes of faith.

When Dr. Cho began his very first church, he had no
money. Services were held in a tent, and there were only
five members. He set up this tent in a slum area because He
believed God had told him he would have a 300-member

church there in the slums. His church was small, but his dream was big. The numbers began to grow. His faith grew. His vision grew.

Dr. Cho would preach to a handful of people in a tiny tent in a very loud voice, as if he was addressing a huge crowd. When his mother-in-law asked him to speak softly and not yell, he replied, "Mother, the people I am speaking to are in the canvas of my heart. In my vision and my dream, I have 10,000 people in my church. So, I am speaking to those 10,000 people."

Dr. Cho explains, "As I see the vision and dream, God fulfills them completely. Vision is seeing your future in your heart. He works from the inside of your heart to your circumstances. You can believe that Jesus Christ loves you or He would never die on the cross for you. Jesus Christ has the power on Heaven and on earth. Trust that you also have His power and you can exercise your faith." [3]

Eyes of Faith

The more we can see the world, our lives, and those around us through the eyes of faith, the more we can align ourselves with God's will and God's plan, by the power of the Holy Spirit. When we ask, God give us eyes of faith, and it gradually changes what we see. We look less and less at things as they presently are, and more and more as they should be—and as they *will* be. We see things, not just the way they are, but the way God intends them to be and the way He promised us they will be one day.

We see brokenness as healing waiting to happen. We see darkness as an invitation to shine a light. We see the lost as waiting for someone to show them the way. We see an enemy as a potential new friend. We see despair as an opportunity to bring hope. We see hatred and racism as the opposition ready to be overwhelmed and abolished by love. We see poverty as the perfect time for God to perform a miracle of multiplication.

> *Every present circumstance will pass,*
> *and only the works of God will last.*

Looking to the Promise

Looking through eyes of faith strengthens our faith, enables us to see how God sees, and empowers us to follow Him closely and to do His works. Fixing our eyes on the promise instead of the present gives us hope that one day our faith will become reality. The perfect example of a person who looked to the promise through eyes of faith and was able to perform the most perfect work of God was, of course, Jesus Christ.

> *Looking unto Jesus, the author and finisher*
> *of our faith, who __for the joy that was set__*
> *__before Him__ endured the cross, despising the*
> *shame, and has sat down at the right hand*
> *of the throne of God.*
> Hebrews 12:2 (emphasis mine)

Jesus endured the horror of the cross *for the joy that was set before Him.* He was not looking at His present painful circumstances which He knew were only temporary. He was looking at the eternal reward which, at that point, could only be seen through eyes of faith. He was looking at the prize which He knew He would receive—being reunited with His Heavenly Father and sitting down at His right hand of glory. That is how Christ "endured the cross, despising the shame." He still experienced tremendous pain, but in the pain and suffering, He fixed His eyes on the eternal unseen reality of God, and He knew it was worth it.

Like Jesus, Moses also endured suffering by looking to the promise. After he left the palace in Egypt he suffered much as a wandering shepherd in the wilderness. Rather than fixing his eyes on what was seen (the passing pleasures of sin and the treasures of Egypt), he looked to the unseen, but eternal reward:

By faith, Moses, when he became of age, refused to be called the son of Pharaoh's daughter, choosing rather to suffer affliction with the people of God than to enjoy the passing pleasures of sin, esteeming the reproach of Christ greater riches than the treasures in Egypt; for he looked to the reward.

Hebrews 11:24-26

Eyes of Faith in the Physical

Without realizing it—and to a much smaller degree—every day, we do just what Jesus and Moses did; we endure temporary suffering for the hopes of future gain. And we also look to the reward with eyes of faith. Some of us work out, eat right, and exercise because *we believe* that it will result in a better, more healthy body in the future. We envision that strong, beautiful body in our minds. We endure long, arduous plane rides because *we believe* the pilot will eventually take us to our desired destination. We envision the places we are traveling in our minds. We work hard, save money, and tithe because *we believe* it will lead to a more prosperous future. With our imaginations, we envision a future of total financial freedom and prosperity.

We believe all these things in the physical world. We see them in our minds through eyes of faith, and we act on them accordingly, as if they were 100% guaranteed. But they are not. We can work-out in the gym for hours a day and still not see the results we want. Exercise and diet do not necessarily mean we will be healthy and disease-free. We can work very hard and save every penny and still wind up bankrupt due to bad investments or health crisis. We only hope the pilot will bring us safely to our destination. Planes can crash, get rerouted due to weather, or (God forbid) they can be hijacked.

We are already doing all these actions by faith and using eyes of faith to envision our desired end. However, it is only faith in our fellow man. It is not faith in God. We have faith in the basic make-up of the human body and the science of good nutrition. We have faith in our economic system in America. We have faith in the pilot and in the aircraft. We have faith in all these things we can taste, see, hear and touch—all of which are only temporary. How much more then should we have faith in the things of God, which are unseen, but eternal?

While the promises of man are good, they are NEVER 100% guaranteed. However, ALL of God's promises and every word He ever speaks is always completely guaranteed, backed by the power of the Almighty One, Who created the entire universe with a breath and a word. If we believe in God at all, why in the world would we not believe in everything He says and does?!

> *For all the promises of God in Him (Christ) are Yes,*
> *and in Him Amen, to the glory of God through us.*
> 2 Corinthians 1:20

When we shift our gaze from the passing present to the unseen eternal reality, then we begin to see the way He sees. We will be able to more clearly see Him at work when we look at the world through eyes of faith. And the better we can see what He is doing presently, the more effectively we can partner with Him right now to change eternity.

In the physical world, "you look before you leap." Sight precedes action. So also, in the spiritual: we look through eyes of faith and act according to what we see. If we fail to see, we fail to act. And clearer sight leads to swifter, more accurate, confident action. We can ask the Father to give us eyes of faith to see how He is already at work all around us. It enables us to do what He does, to participate in His eternal work. Jesus practiced this principle flawlessly. He watched His Father closely and only did what He saw the Father doing:

The Son can do nothing of Himself, but what He sees the Father do; for whatever He does, the Son also does in like manner.
John 5:19

Eyes of Faith for Healing

"What are you believing God for today?" Tom asked one morning as we waited with our team in the hotel lobby. We were waiting for the van to take us to the clinic site.

Our medical team was three days in on a two-week mission trip to Myanmar. We were already in full swing and comfortable in our daily routines, as well as with each other. I stopped for a moment to ponder his intriguing question. I thought about what the Holy Spirit had been impressing on my heart and what I could see God doing that day through my own eyes of faith. I replied: "I suppose I'm believing God will do a miracle healing today involving eyes—restoring sight for someone."

"I'll agree with that!" Tom said with a smile.

As the day wore on, I kept an expectant eye out for patients with total loss of vision, determined to pray for anyone who was blind. Tom did the same and he sent them my way. I began to suspect God was up to something good. About halfway through the day, Marcus, another team member who was fitting patients with eyeglasses, came over to the medical clinic where I was working. He introduced me to Win, a young man in his 20s who had congenital cataracts in his left eye. His right eye had good vision, but his left eye had been almost completely blind for about ten years. This was difficult for him because he was a driver by profession and relied heavily on his right eye. As a poor man in a poor country, surgery was not an option. Win told us the vision in his left eye was so bad he could not even see the skin color of the person sitting directly in front of him. All he could see was a blur of light. One of our doctors assessed him and confirmed it was cataracts. There was nothing we could do.

I realized this could be an opportunity for the Holy Spirit to move. I led Win downstairs to a quiet place to pray, joined by Tom and a Burmese translator. Through the translator, we talked to Win about the Lord and asked permission to pray for him. Win confessed that his father was a Christian and he had heard the message of the gospel. But he had been running from God for quite some time. He called himself the "black sheep" of his family. We shared with Win about the deep love, limitless forgiveness, and restoring power of God. He was very open to receive the Lord and definitely open to receive healing.

We explained that the blood of Jesus could wash him white as snow; that he didn't have to be a black sheep; that the Lord could forgive his sins and heal his body. Win said that was what he wanted, so I led him in a simple prayer of salvation to receive the Lord Jesus Christ as his Savior. Then, I led him in a second prayer to receive Jesus as his Healer. I anointed him with oil of frankincense, and we prayed for total restoration of sight in his blind eye.

After praying, we asked Win what he felt. He said he felt peace inside, and he also felt something changing in his left eye. We examined his eye. It seemed to be clearing a little and the pupils appeared to be more equal and reactive. "It's working!" I said, "Let's do it again!"

We prayed again. Then, I asked him to cover his good eye so we could test the vision in his bad eye. When he did this, Win was surprised and told us he could see the Burmese translator sitting directly in front of him. For the first time he could see the color of his skin with his bad eye, though it was still blurry. "What color is his skin?" I asked.

"Same color as me!" He shouted, laughing.

We prayed again. Next, I decided to test his vision using a simple finger test. I held up two fingers in front of his face while he covered his good eye with his right hand.

"How many fingers?" I asked.

"Two." Win replied.

I took a few steps back and held up three.

"How many fingers?" I asked.

"Three." He replied.

This time I stood in the far back corner of the room and held up four.

"How many fingers?"

"Four!" He shouted, still covering his good eye and looking only through his bad eye. We cheered, clapped, and celebrated, giving thanks and praise to God for restoring Win's sight. Win was all smiles and said he had "new eyes." He knew his sight had come from Jesus. He told us he was going to follow Christ and be a "black sheep" no longer. God restored his physical sight as well as his spiritual sight. My own faith was strengthened and perhaps a father's prayer for his wandering son was also answered on that day. Luckily for Win, the Heavenly Father is still in the business of opening blind eyes.

The Lord opens the eyes of the blind; the Lord raises up those who are bowed down; the Lord loves the righteous.

Psalm 146:8

See the Unseen

Eyes of faith can show us what is happening in the spiritual realm in our present world. My mother was once fervently praying for a young boy who was very sick. While she prayed, God gave her a beautiful vision of a golden staircase leading up to heaven, with angels singing while traveling up and down the stairs. She later discovered that her vision came at the exact time the little boy passed away. God was revealing the reality of what was happening in the spiritual realm. God gives us eyes of faith to see the unseen; to see what He sees.

One morning, long, long ago, Elisha, the prophet of God in Israel, was surrounded by the army of the King of Syria. When Elisha's servant went out and saw the army encamped against them, he panicked and ran to his master. Elisha responded, "Do not fear, for those who are with us are more than those who are with them" (2 Kings 6:16). Then Elisha prayed and asked God to open the physical eyes of his fearful servant. The Lord opened the servant's eyes, and this is what he saw: "Behold, the mountain was full of horses and chariots of fire all around Elisha" (2 Kings 6:17). Elisha had eyes of faith to see the unseen chariots of fire and the great army of the Lord. Elisha saw and acknowledged the army of the king of Syria with his physical eyes. But he also saw the army of the Lord and he knew it was greater.

In our lives today, when we find ourselves surrounded by the enemy's armies, we don't have to see the angels of fire and the armies of the Lord with our physical eyes. Like Elisha, we can see them through eyes of faith. We know for certain the Lord's armies are with us and are much stronger than the enemy. We know this because He told us: "He who is in you is greater than he who is in the world" (1 John 4:4).

Faith Looks Forward

One thing I do, forgetting those things which are behind and reaching forward to those things which are ahead, I press on toward the goal for the prize of the upward call of God in Christ Jesus.
Philippians 3:13-14

In the wonderful world of horses, there is a saying that every good equestrian knows: *Always look where you want to go.* The horse is an extremely sensitive animal and can feel the slightest movement and shift of weight in your body, even the tilting of your head. The horse intuitively knows where you are looking and will be inclined to go in that direction. You must look forward to move forward. If you're moving forward but looking back, you're sure to crash!

We will always move in the direction we fix our gaze.

Faith looks forward and moves forward. By faith, we look forward to where we want to go with God. We resist the temptation to look back and long for the past. A classic example of the dangers of looking back is the story of Lot and his family. They were rescued by two angels from the destruction of Sodom and Gomorrah, two exceedingly wicked cities God was about to destroy with fire. While they were escaping, the angels told them not to look back at the city where they lived. According to the scripture, Lot's wife did not obey; she looked back and was instantly turned into a pillar of salt (Genesis 19).

Jesus himself taught that anyone who begins to move forward, but then looks back, is not fit for the Kingdom of God (Luke 9:62). If we look back, we will go back. The writer of Hebrews warned that even if the heroes of faith who were seeking a "heavenly country" were to look back, then they would have opportunity to return to the bondage of Egypt:

> *And truly if they had called to mind that country from which they had come out, they would have had opportunity to return. But now, they desire a better, that is, a heavenly country. Therefore, God is not ashamed to be called their God, for He has prepared a city for them.*
> Hebrews 11:15-16

Faith only looks back briefly in times of remembrance of the wonderful things the Lord has done; to rejoice and increase the faith of ourselves and others by proclaiming the great works of God. Times of recollection are helpful and good, but faith does not dwell on the past. It looks forward at what God is doing next and presses on to the promises of God for the future.

When God is doing something new (and He is always doing something new), He instructs us not to look back at the past and dwell on the works of old, whether good or bad, but rather to look forward at what He is about to do, so we don't miss it:

Do not remember the former things, nor consider the things of old. Look, I will do a new thing, now it shall spring forth; shall you not know it?
Isaiah 43:18-19

Look to Jesus

In my travels overseas, I have come across more than one testimony of a believer who claims he was blind (or at least partially blind), and when he met Jesus, He healed his eyes and gave him sight. These are always encouraging and inspiring stories. Each story is different, but each believer had this in common: *they looked to Jesus.*

Looking unto Jesus, the author and finisher of our faith...
Hebrews 12:2

There is no better place to continually fix our gaze than on Jesus Christ Himself, the Captain of our faith. May we never leave His side. Throughout the ages, there are countless examples for us to follow—men and women of faith, looking to Jesus in every circumstance:

- Peter looked to Jesus as he walked on the waves in the storm. (Matthew 14:29)

- The woman caught in adultery looked to Jesus for forgiveness. (John 8:1-11)

- The Israelites looked to the bronze serpent (a foreshadowing of Jesus) for healing. (Numbers 21:9, John 3:14)

- Shadrach, Meshach, and Abednego looked to Jesus inside the fiery furnace. (Daniel 3:25)

- Hungry multitudes of men and women looked to Jesus for food. (Matthew 14:15-21)

- Mary and Martha looked to Jesus for a miracle for their brother Lazarus. (John 11:1-44)

- The thief on the cross looked to Jesus for salvation. (Luke 23:39-43)

- Nicodemus looked to Jesus to learn how to be born again. (John 3:1-21)

- Mary, His mother, looked to Jesus to provide wine at the wedding in Cana. (John 2:1-10)

- The demon possessed man looked to Jesus for deliverance and a sound mind. (Mark 5:1-15)

- Stephen looked to Jesus as he was being stoned to death because of his faith. (Acts 7:55-56)

- Saul, the killer of Christians, looked to Jesus and became the Apostle Paul. (Acts 9:1-19)

For every person that has ever looked to Jesus,
He has never failed them yet . . .

CHAPTER EIGHT

WHAT HAPPENS
WHEN FAITH FAILS?

*In this you greatly rejoice, though now for a little while,
if need be, you have been grieved by various trials, that
the genuineness of your faith, being much more precious
than gold that perishes, though it is tested by fire...*
1 Peter 1:6-7

Of all the things I have heard and seen, if there was
ever a room of women "tested by fire," this was it. I was in
Liberia, Africa, half-way through a nine-month stint with
Mercy Ships. Nothing could have prepared me for what I
was about to behold.

Along with some other women from the ship, I had
the privilege of visiting one of Mother Teresa's Home for
the Sick and the Dying. When we entered the high-walled
compound, I was struck by the beauty, tranquility, and
presence of Jesus. I still don't understand how, but it felt
like there was a soft light radiating everywhere—almost as

if light was shining off the dark walls in the middle of the night. There were flowers, a fountain, a large statue of Jesus outside, and beautiful pictures and scriptures inside. The happy sisters who greeted us had bright eyes and cheerful smiles. These sisters escorted us into the main room which housed the women living in this beautiful compound. There were nearly 20 young African women. Some were healthy-looking, others were nearing death's door. Some had infants next to their beds, others sat alone. All of them—including the babies—were dying of AIDS.

After the AIDS epidemic spread across Africa, a horrible myth began to take root in many countries—that the cure for AIDS was for a man to have sex with a virgin girl. Many of these women and their sick babies were victims of that terrible lie.

I sat down on a bed, and one of the women promptly handed me her baby. As I held that little one, who was too weak to cry, and gazed at the faces of those strong, beautiful women now facing early death, I was overwhelmed. I began to weep for them. But it wasn't long before I realized I was the only one crying. One of the African women pulled out a Bible and read from Job. She explained that they were not sad, so I shouldn't cry either. Instead, they were all happy because they knew they were like Job, and soon they were all going to be with Jesus. So, every day at lunchtime, they have a celebration service. And we had arrived just in time.

They started with a happy song of thanksgiving, called "Tell Papa God Tankee." This is Liberian for "Tell God Thank You." The women who could still walk stood up with African tambourines and drums and danced around the room joyfully. I was amazed. The next song touched me so deeply, that I still remember it. These are the words those beautiful women sang:

Problems. I will give God my problems.
If I give God my problems, He will take care of me.
He will never ever let me down. I will give God my
problems. Children. I will give God my children.
If I give God my children, He will take care of them.
He will never ever let me down. I will give God my
children. My whole life. I will give God my whole life.
If I give God my whole life, He will take care of me . . .

On and on they went as they laughed and danced around the room. The ones who couldn't get out of bed were smiling and clapping. The sisters were meeting their physical needs, and God was doing the rest. At first glance, it seemed that faith had failed them; that prayers were unanswered; that the enemy had won. After all, these were innocent young women suffering and dying alongside their precious little babies. But that wasn't true at all.

Modern medicine perhaps had failed them,
but their faith had saved them.

There was more joy, peace, light, love, happiness, and complete Christian fellowship in that room than almost any other place I have seen, before or since. Their faith was tried and tested by the hot fires of rape, disease, and death. Now they were all shining like solid gold; praising God constantly; waiting to go Home to receive their reward. Each one was a different jewel in a priceless heavenly crown. They knew where they were going, and they were ready. They were not afraid to face death. Their faith did not fail them at all. It gave them victory.

> *Death is swallowed up in victory. O Death, where is your sting? O Grave, where is your victory?*
> 1 Corinthians 15:54-55

Faith Under Fire

While the women in Africa tried their faith in the fires of life, there were three great men long ago, who walked through literal fires, and survived because of their faith.

Shadrach, Meshach, and Abednego were three Hebrew men who only worshiped God. However, they worked for king Nebuchadnezzar of Babylon, who only worshiped his own idols. When the king made a giant gold image and commanded everyone to bow down and worship it, these three brave men of God refused. Nebuchadnezzar was enraged and ordered Shadrach, Meshach, and Abednego to be cast into a fiery furnace if they would not bow down in worship (Daniel 3:1-15). This was their reply:

If that is the case, our God whom we serve is able
to deliver us from the burning fiery furnace, and He will
deliver us from your hand, O king. But if not, let it be known
to you, O king, that we do not serve your gods, nor will
we worship the gold image which you have set up.
Daniel 3:17-18

The faith of Shadrach, Meshach, and Abednego was an unwavering, unshakable faith in God alone, regardless of the outcome. When they asked God to deliver them, they were placing their faith in who He is, in His powerful nature and loving character. They knew that He *could*. They believed that He *would*. But at the end of the day, He is God alone, and it's His call. So even if He didn't save them, they were still prepared to walk through the fire because of their faith.

Whether they were delivered from the flames or not, their faith could not fail them. They knew that if God had not rescued them, He would still be God and He would still be good. They would have died swiftly with their bodies burned up, but their faith unbroken. And to them, it was worth it.

Faith is not just a means to an end. Faith is the end.

Faith itself is far more valuable than any fire we could ever endure; any mountain that could ever be moved; any promise we could ever receive; any prayer we could ever pray. It is faith that pleases God. And God was pleased with the faith of Shadrach, Meshach, and Abednego. In the end, He did deliver them safely out of the fiery furnace. And king Nebuchadnezzar blessed and extolled their God (Daniel 3:19-30).

When Dreams Die

> *To everything there is a season, a time for every purpose under heaven; a time to be born, and a time to die..*
> Ecclesiastes 3:1-2

Because God loves us so much more than we can comprehend, sometimes a dream must die. Not because it wasn't good, but because *it wasn't good enough*. The Father never likes to see His children hurting and suffering loss. Still, in His love, He allows it to happen, but only for a greater good—to bring something even better into our lives. From our perspective, the very thing we were hoping and praying and believing God for is the very thing that He takes away. It hurts deeply. But from His perspective, it is not cruelty. It is amazing grace, unfailing love, and astounding goodness, that has only yet to be fully revealed to us. The Father's deep desire and joy is that we delight in Him, so that He may fulfill His word and satisfy ALL the desires of our hearts (Psalm 37:4) in far better ways than we can ever ask or imagine!

After all, He is the Greatest Giver who gives without measure and promises to withhold *no good thing* from those who walk uprightly (Psalm 84:11). When we do not receive what we are asking and seeking, it's not because He isn't good; *it's because He is!* When our dreams for our lives do not line up with His dreams for us, eventually our dreams *must die*, because He only wants us to have the very best and nothing less. God causes everything (the good, the bad, and the ugly) to work together in our lives for one primary purpose: that we may be like Christ . . . perfect and complete, lacking nothing (1 John 3:2, James 1:4).

Even when we have disappointments, dashed hopes, broken dreams, or unanswered prayers, we can take solace in the promise that those are the times when the Good Shepherd draws near to comfort and restore. When He comes, bringing hope and healing in His wings, all sorrow vanishes, and we remember the pain no more.

> *The Lord is near to those who have a broken heart*
> *and saves such as have a contrite spirit.*
> Psalm 34:11

When dreams die, we hurt. We cry. We may be tempted to lose faith. But we do not lose faith. Because our faith was never in the dream itself. We do not place our faith in the outcome we are dictating to God. We place our faith in God alone.

Like Shadrach, Meshach, and Abednego, we place our faith in His character, in who He is. And *who He is* is always unbelievably good. Then, like Job, the righteous man who suddenly lost everything for no apparent reason, we can learn to say:

The Lord gives, and the Lord takes away.
Blessed be the name of the Lord.
Job 1:21

When we find ourselves in this place, we can follow Job who, "did not sin and did not charge God with wrongdoing" (Job 1:22). We can start again in faith, waiting on the promises of God, trusting in His character. Because He always restores, and He will bring about something much greater than anything we had in mind. We can exchange our dreams for God's dreams, which are infinitely better. In the end, Job received far more than he lost. God restored all of Job's losses and gave him twice as much as he had before (Job 42:10-17).

When it feels like faith has failed us, sometimes it is only a matter of perspective. And in time, when God reveals the whole picture, we will see that faith never fails. It cannot fail, because faith is always victorious. Faith is the victory that conquers the world (1 John 5:4).

Waiting in Faith

These all died in faith, not having received the promises,
but having seen them afar off were assured of them,
embraced them and confessed that they were
strangers and pilgrims on the earth.

Hebrews 11:13

If we find ourselves waiting in faith, believing God for a promise that has never come to pass, at least we can be sure of this: *We are in good company!* Noah, Abraham, Sarah, Isaac, Jacob, Joseph, Moses, and many others were waiting for promises from God that were not fulfilled until after they died. And in some cases, it was hundreds of years after they died! That means even in Heaven, they still had to wait a very long time to see the fulfillment on earth.

When they didn't see God's word fulfilled in their own lifetimes, it may have appeared that faith had failed them, that God did not keep His word. But they didn't doubt God. They could see the promises afar off with eyes of faith. They were *assured of them*, *embraced them*, and never stopped believing—even in death.

Now we look back on the pages of history and we see—they were right! God was faithful. Every promise came to pass. Every word was fulfilled. He was faithful to them. He is faithful to us. His word is always true. It never ever fails. When we place our faith in God and in His Word, it cannot fail. When everything else fails and passes away, *faith will remain . . .*

CHAPTER NINE

THESE THREE REMAIN

And now, these three remain: faith, hope, and love;
but the greatest of these is love.
1 Corinthians 13:13

When the miracle is over, and the answered prayers have passed; when the mountain that moved and left us amazed is long forgotten, along with all the wonderful people we met and the exotic places we traveled; when every tongue is silenced; when the curtain comes down and the lights of the world go dim; then, only these three things will remain: Faith. Hope. Love.

Asking Prayer is rooted in hope. Believing Prayer is rooted in faith. Both are very good and very necessary for salvation, sanctification, and redemption of all people. But, as it turns out, of these three: *Love is the greatest*. Without love, there would be no faith and no hope. There would be no prayer at all. Because love is the foundation of prayer. Neither Asking Prayer nor Believing Prayer would exist without love. Without love, there would be nothing to have faith in, nothing to hope for, and certainly no one to pray to. Because God is love (1 John 4:8).

For God so loved the world that He gave
His one and only Son, that whosoever believes in
Him will not perish but have eternal life.
John 3:16

The love of God is displayed most poignantly on the cross, which brings the hope of salvation through faith. But that is not all. His great love is woven throughout the entire story of mankind—from Genesis to Revelation—just as Jesus is the "author and finisher" of our faith (Heb 12:2) . . .

God is the author and finisher of Love.

Everything God has ever done, and everything He will ever do, is an act of pure love. Creation, revelation, justification, crucifixion, resurrection, redemption, adoption, salvation, sanctification, and glorification—all of it is done in love, by love, for love, and because of love. The magnificent love of God is the pen that has carefully sketched the history of all creation, from the dawning of the first day to the setting of the last sun. God's love was and is and will forever be with us. It is as infinite as Himself. Faith is greater than hope. But love is greater than faith.

Faith is the force that brings victory in the world,
but Love is the One who made it.

All love comes from God, and we only love because He loved us first (1 John 4:19). The love we have because of God deserves to be given back to God. Christ demonstrated ultimate love by laying down His own life for us and calling us His friends (John 15:13). He asks us to do the same, to lay down our lives every day because of our love for Him and to follow Him for the sake of the Kingdom of God. The Father gave us love so we can give it back to Him.

Love for God is the first and greatest commandment. And love for your neighbor is second. Jesus said if we can only succeed in following these two commands, (loving God and loving people) we will essentially fulfill the entire Law of God (Matthew 22:37-40). God knew long ago that we would fall short. That's why He sent Jesus to redeem us and the Holy Spirit to teach and empower us. He knew our need for love was huge. But we needed much more than just instruction and inspiration to learn how to love like He loves.

We needed a *heart transplant*. And that's exactly what He did:

> *I will give you a new heart and put a*
> *new spirit within you; I will take the heart of*
> *stone out of your flesh and give you a heart of flesh.*
> Ezekiel 36:26

He said those words thousands of years ago, and they are still just as true today as the day they were written. God is still in the business of changing hearts and transforming lives.

Transformed by Love

The love of God carries tremendous transforming power. It changes people. Oftentimes, this transforming love of God is received directly from the hands and hearts of other people. I watched this kind of love while I was serving God in Liberia, Africa. There I witnessed the total transformation—body, soul, and spirit—of a young man named Bowa.

One hot African day, Bowa arrived on the Mercy Ship, where I was serving as a nurse. As he entered the medical ward, his face was completely covered with a bright African headwrap. All anyone could see were his eyes. And those downcast eyes were filled with sorrow and shame.

Bowa was suffering from a large tumor, roughly the size of a football, which had grown out of his jaw and deformed his face. Although it was benign, it was certainly life-altering, and would eventually be fatal. This tumor had grown so large it was compressing his esophagus and would likely close off his airway if left unchecked; and it was impossible for him to swallow anything other than liquids and soft pureed foods. Bowa was slowly starving to death.

To make matters worse, he lived in a country where superstition reigns supreme over faith, love, and logic. Bowa's neighbors were afraid of him. Some said he was cursed by witch doctors. Some said he was punished by God. Others believed his unfortunate malady was contagious. They were quick to condemn and quick to shun. He could no longer defend himself because he had lost the ability to speak. Bowa lived an isolated life, was completely rejected and hidden away from the world.

Bowa stayed with us on the ward for several days while waiting for his life-saving operation. The surgeons on board the Mercy Ship would remove the tumor and perform total reconstructive surgery. During that time, the nurses gave Bowa an endless supply of protein shakes and blended meals, which he gratefully accepted before crawling underneath a blanket behind his bed to hide. He was so ashamed, he didn't want anyone to see him eat.

When Bowa's big day arrived, he seemed frightened and excited at the same time. After several hours in the OR, he returned to us wrapped up in bandages—and tumor free. Due to the size and depth of his massive tumor, Bowa would need to have several surgeries for reconstruction: bone grafting, skin grafting, and extensive wound care. This required him to stay with us for a few months.

That is when the real transformation began. As the surgeons skillfully patched Bowa's face back together, God was tenderly patching up his battered heart. The nurses, patients, chaplains, and other volunteers on the ship showed up every day to shower Bowa with compassion and love. Little by little, he came out of hiding. He started smiling, joking, playing games with the nurses, and dancing to the African drums during worship time on the ward. As the weeks went by, Bowa had to relearn how to speak and how to eat. And along the way, he also learned how to live, to laugh, and to love.

By the time he left us, Bowa was a new man with a new face and new heart. He had been transformed by love. He received the love of God and accepted Christ as his Savior. Perhaps for the first time in his life, Bowa had peace in his soul, joy in his heart, and big smile on his face.

In different ways and to different degrees, we are all just like Bowa. It is Love that transforms all of us.

That love originates only from the God of Love, who is always looking for ways to pour out His love into our hearts. And He wants us, in turn, to look for ways to pour out our love into the lives of other thirsty souls. Sometimes, He places someone like Bowa in our path, so we can learn how to love like He loves. And when we love, we find ourselves changed. We become a little more like Him. We love because He first loved us (1 John 4:19).

Do you love Me?

In one of the final interactions Jesus had with Peter on this earth, He asked him a telling question that cuts to the heart, and grieved Peter's heart. Jesus followed it with a command for Peter to do what He had called him to do all along. Some say that perhaps Jesus repeats the question three times because that was the number of times Peter denied Him. Thus, Jesus was giving Peter a chance to redeem himself. It could also be that Jesus repeats it three times to emphasize the importance of the question, as was often done in that culture. Either way, it is definitely a question of utmost importance. It made all the difference for Peter and it makes all the difference for us. It is a question every person should ask themselves about Jesus in all honesty and sincerity: *Do you love Me?*

> *When they had eaten breakfast, Jesus said to Simon Peter,*
> *"Simon, son of Jonah, do you love Me more than these?"*
> *He said to Him, "Yes, Lord; You know that I love You."*
> *He said to him, "Feed My lambs." He said to him*
> *again a second time, "Simon, son of Jonah,*
> *do you love Me?" He said to Him, "Yes, Lord;*
> *You know that I love You." He said to him,*
> *"Tend My sheep." He said to him the third time,*
> *"Simon, son of Jonah, do you love Me?" Peter*
> *was grieved because he said to him the third time,*
> *"Do you love Me?"and he said to Him,*
> *"Lord, You know all things; You know that I love You."*
> *Jesus said to him, "Feed My sheep."*
> John 21:15-17

Love for Jesus Christ is the true mark of salvation.

Love is the sign which hangs on the hearts of all God's children, no matter their background, education, denomination or upbringing. The hearts of all sincere believers burn with love for the Father, the Son, and the Holy Spirit. It is not enough just to believe that He exists. The Bible says even the demons have faith! They believe

God exists. They know Jesus is His son, and they fear Him (James 2:19). But they certainly do not love Him.

Jesus said there will be many people who will do many great things in His name who will not enter His Kingdom (Matthew 7:21-23). These people did amazing signs and wonders in His name. They claimed to be His followers. However, we know they did not really know Him, and they did not really love Him, because they did not obey Him. They had faith enough to call Him "Lord," but they lacked love and obedience. And He will say to them, "I never knew you. Depart from Me, you who practice lawlessness!" (Matthew 7:23). To know Him, to really know Him, is to love Him. If you do not love Him, you do not know Him. If you love Him, you obey Him.

Ask in faith. Abide in love. Act in obedience.

A child, if he is lucky enough to be born into a loving family with loving parents, does not ever have to be instructed or taught to love his father and mother. It is in his nature to love them. Indeed, before he even began to love them, they loved him first. They gave him life. They provide for all his needs. They demonstrate their love to their child in a million ways.

When a person becomes "born-again" into the family of God, they are given a new nature, a new heart. And just like the child cannot help but love his parents, the child of God cannot help but to love and worship and adore his Heavenly Father, who also demonstrates His love daily— in a million different ways.

I have not seen a more beautiful expression of such a sincere, deep love and adoration for God than what I saw one winter day from the heart and lips of a simple, uneducated homeless man in Nashville, Tennessee.

During one season of my life, I was part of an amazing small-group. Our group leader, Ben Gatrelle, had met an older man (whom I will call Jon) who was homeless most of his life and was just transitioning off the street into an apartment not far from Ben's house. Ben invited Jon to visit our little Bible study, which was held in Ben's home, and he came.

After introductions, we went around the circle as each person read aloud a portion of Acts 3, the story where Peter healed the lame man. When it was Jon's turn, he told us he had never learned how to read. So, we read his portion for him out loud while he listened. We asked what he thought about the Bible story and this was his reply:

> That's a real nice story. I like it a lot. Especially because, that was me. I was that lame man! This is my story. It happened to me. I used to have terrible gout in my knees and ankles. It hurt so bad I couldn't walk. One day, I was sittin' on the curb. A woman came by and said, "Why are you just sittin' there?" I said, "Well ma'am, I'm sittin' here, 'cause I cain't walk." She says, "If Jesus can heal you and make you walk again, will you come with me to my church picnic?" Seeing as I had nowhere else to be and nothing else to do, I said I would. She said those same words to me that you just read: "In the name of Jesus, get up and

walk," and then I did! All my pain was gone, and it never came back to this day. I went with that lady to the church picnic. That's where I found Jesus and got saved. He healed me. He saved me. He got me off the streets and turned my life around.

We were all quite surprised (to say the least!) and thanked him for sharing this very unexpected, inspiring story. As we continued the Bible study we began to talk about Heaven and the assurance of salvation for believers. This is when Jon surprised us even further. He said he wasn't sure he was going to Heaven at all, because of all the bad things he had done in his past.

Ben read some scripture to Jon to reassure him that because he had accepted Christ in his heart and was genuinely saved, he was completely forgiven and was surely going to be in Heaven. Again, Jon resisted, saying he may or may not make it to Heaven when he died. Nothing we could say seemed to convince him at all. I will never forget Jon's explanation that day:

I don't know much of what's in that book; because, like I told you before, I can't read. But I do know this: I done a lot of bad things in my life and I don't deserve Heaven. Maybe God will forgive me, maybe not. I wouldn't blame Him if He didn't. But He healed me, and He saved me, and He got me off the streets. So, I just love Him, and I thank Him, and I praise Him every day, because He is good. He's just so good. The truth is, no matter what that book says, at the end of the day, it is **His Heaven**, not mine. **He is God**, not me. He can do whatever He wants. Ain't NOBODY gonna stop Him!! So, it's His call, whoever He's gonna let into His house. And when I die, and stand before the gates, if He says, *Sorry Jon, you didn't make it*, and He decides not to let me in. Well then, I guess I'll go to hell . . . But as soon as I get there, I'm just gonna love Him, and I'm gonna thank Him, and I'm gonna praise Him every day. Because, He's good. He's just so good. And He deserves it.

Ben smiled wisely at Jon's humble insistence that he may not make it to Heaven, and he replied: "Well, Jon, if you were to go to hell, I guarantee this: You would be the only one there loving Jesus and thanking and praising God! I can't imagine God would ever let that happen."

I never saw Jon again. But I will never forget him, and I'm certain I'll see him one day.

In His days on earth, Jesus understood this kind of reckless, selfless extravagant love from grateful sinners, just like Jon. "The one who is forgiven much, also loves much" (Luke 7:47). Jon's simple yet powerful, unquestioning love and adoration for his God is a love worth imitating. Jon never read a single word from the book that commands us to love God. But somehow, as soon as he met Jesus and became a child of God, he could not help but to love, praise, worship, and adore the Lord of Glory. Jon got it right.

We love Him, and we thank Him, and we praise Him every day, no matter what, for this reason:

Because He is good. He is just so good. And He deserves our praise.

What matters more than miracles, than mountains moved, and answered prayers; what matters even more than faith; what matters most in life—is what lies in the heart of man. Do we love Him? Do we really love Him?

It is Love Who gave His life for us,
and Love will bring us Home.

About the Author

Caroline Chesnutt is a registered nurse, specializing in the medical ICU. Initially, her desire to become a nurse was solely for the purpose of doing medical mission work abroad. Caroline began her walk with Jesus Christ while in college at Texas Tech University. There, she developed a passion for foreign missions through Campus Crusade for Christ and has been participating in mission work ever since. She has traveled to more countries than she can count and enjoyed more adventures than she can believe. She also lived in Africa for two years serving with Mercy Ships on board the Africa Mercy.

Since 2010, Caroline has been serving the Lord doing short-term medical mission trips with Health Teams International mission organization. She actively serves on the board with Health Teams International and is working with them to bring the gospel of Jesus Christ to the last remaining unreached peoples of the world. Second only to pursuing a closer walk with God, reaching the unreached is her primary passion and goal in life. Caroline currently resides just outside of Nashville, Tennessee in a cozy little cabin with her two beautiful horses, Tiger and Hillary.

About Health Teams International

Health Teams International (HTI) is a group of international Evangelical Christians with no dues or membership or church affiliation, just people from all walks of life who desire to follow Jesus' command to go into all the world and preach the Gospel.

HTI was incorporated 35 years ago with our constitution and by-laws stating we are to go only to the unreached people groups of the world. It is estimated that there are between eleven and twelve thousand people groups left on earth who still have never heard the name of Jesus Christ. These people have no church, no viable witness, and no access to the gospel.

HTI goes into countries where we are invited by in-country pastors, evangelists, and missionaries who have been trying to reach these unreached people mostly by verbally sharing the Gospel. These local believers serve as our hosts. By partnering with HTI, there have been great results and much fruit in every country. When we demonstrate meaningful Christian love to the unreached with much needed medical, dental, and optical care, suddenly, their ears and hearts are open to hear the Gospel.

In our 35 years of service, HTI has seen over 150,000 unreached people choose to accept Jesus Christ and become Christians. These people are then connected to the local believers and missionaries for discipleship and growth. This model of evangelism has been very effective.

Most of our teams are made up of healthcare professionals. However, we always need some lay people for tasks such as fitting eyeglasses and sorting medications, as well as evangelism and prayer. I usually warn first time team members that their experience can be addicting because over 90% of our team members return. It is personally very rewarding to experience the joy of offering both hands of the gospel to the world's poorest people who have no access to the gospel: bringing much needed healthcare, and the saving message of Jesus Christ. We hope you will consider joining us in finishing the task of bringing the Gospel to every nation, as Jesus commanded.

Richard E. Charlick, D.D.S., M.S.
President / CEO Health Teams International

This Gospel of the Kingdom will be preached to all the nations, and then the end will come.
Matthew 24:14

NOTES

(1) Chapter 4: Grace Honduras – Grace Honduras Ministry is still in operation and serving the people of the dump. They are always in need of donations, funds, and volunteers. If you would like to get more information, donate, or get involved, you can contact the ministry at: www.gracehonduras.org, gracehonduras@gmail.com

Katherine Melissa Mejia at: katherinemejiam23@gmail.com

Kristin Milhizer Allen, USA, fundraising coordinator at: kristinallen1970@gmail.com

(2) Chapter 5: Maury Davis has now retired. His son, Galen Davis, is currently the leading pastor of Cornerstone Nashville Church in Madison, TN, which is growing, thriving, and bringing great glory to God. www.cornerstonenashville.org

(3) Chapter 7: http://christianitymalaysia.com/wp/god-wants-you-to-have-a-vision-and-a-dream-dr-yonggi-cho-of-yoido-full-gospel-church-korea/